S0-FMJ-903

STUDIES IN THE GERMANIC LANGUAGES AND LITERATURES
Number 4

EDITORIAL COMMITTEE

Norman H. Binger   John Wesley Thomas
Bernd Kratz   Paul K. Whitaker
Ingeborg H. Solbrig   A. Wayne Wonderley *(chairman)*

THE TALES AND SONGS OF
HERRAND VON WILDONIE

THE TALES AND SONGS
OF
HERRAND VON WILDONIE

TRANSLATED INTO ENGLISH VERSE
WITH AN INTRODUCTION

BY

J. W. THOMAS

THE UNIVERSITY PRESS OF KENTUCKY
LEXINGTON, 1972

STANDARD BOOK NUMBER 0-8131-1267-2
LIBRARY OF CONGRESS CATALOG CARD NUMBER 76-183354

COPYRIGHT © 1972 BY THE UNIVERSITY PRESS OF KENTUCKY

A statewide cooperative scholarly publishing agency serving Berea College, Centre College of Kentucky, Eastern Kentucky University, Kentucky State College, Morehead State University, Murray State University, University of Kentucky, University of Louisville, and Western Kentucky University

EDITORIAL AND SALES OFFICES: LEXINGTON, KENTUCKY 40506

PRINTED IN SPAIN

DEPÓSITO LEGAL: V. 3.512 - 1972

ARTES GRÁFICAS SOLER, S. A. — JÁVEA, 28 — VALENCIA (8) — 1972

CONTENTS

Page

INTRODUCTION

    The Life of Herrand II von Wildonie 9
    The Tales 14
    The Songs 31

THE TALES

    The Faithful Wife 37
    The Deceived Husband 45
    The Naked Emperor 55
    The Cat 73

THE SONGS

    Song 1 83
    Song 2 84
    Song 3 86

INTRODUCTION

The Life of Herrand II von Wildonie

ON THE RIGHT BANK of the Mur River about twelve miles south of Graz lies the town of Wildon, named for one of the most important families of thirteenth-century Styria. Part way up the mountain above the town one can still see the ruins of the ancestral castle of the knights of Wildonie. It is not known when the castle ceased to be inhabited, but a sketch made in 1681 shows that it was rather well preserved at that time and that it was surrounded by a massive complex of outworks and walls which covered most of the mountain.

The recorded history of the House of Wildonie [1] dates from 1173, when one Hertnidus de Wildonia signed a document as a witness for the ruler of Styria, Margrave Ottacker VIII of Traungau. However, the relationship of this Hertnidus to later members of the family has not been established. The known genealogy, therefore, begins a year later with the grandfather of the poet, who is mentioned in a letter of 1174 and whose name in its Latin form, Herrandus de Wildonia, appears on legal documents from 1180 to 1222. These show him to be an important figure and a close associate of Margrave Ottacker and his successors, the Babenberg Dukes Leopold V and Leopold VI. His official title, Lord High Chamberlain of Styria, was passed down to his grandson and great-grandson.

There is only one record — a letter from one abbot to another — which tells much about the character of this first Herrand von Wildonie, but it is quite revealing about the rude times in which

---

[1] The following biographical information is taken largely from Karl Ferdinand Kummer, "Das Ministerialengeschlecht von Wildonie," *Archiv für österreichische Geschichte* 59 (1880): 177-322.

he lived and the violent disposition that his descendants inherited. The letter deals with Herrand's courtship and marriage. He and Wilhelm von Heunburg forcibly seized two daughters of Baron Leutold von Gutenberg and defeated the troops which the father and his friends led to rescue them, capturing fifty knights in the battle. Archbishop Adelbert of Salzburg brought about a settlement of the dispute by persuading Baron Leutold to agree to the marriage of his daughters to their abductors, and this apparently took place in the latter part of 1174. Herrand's wife brought to her husband considerable property, which served in part as the basis for the important position which he and his heirs subsequently held in the affairs of the duchy. Other records tell of Herrand's seizure of various pieces of land, especially from monasteries, but they also show some generous grants to the Church. As one of his philanthropic enterprises he introduced the order of the Maltese Knights into Styria and gave it a liberal endowment.

Only two of Herrand's four sons were living at the time of his death in about 1222. These were Ulrich (the father of the poet) and Leutold. The brothers usually appear together in the records of the period, which show them once in the company of Emperor Friedrich II and frequently among the retinue of Duke Friedrich II of Austria and Styria. Their relations to the latter may have become strained during the last years of his reign, for no document of the period 1244-1246 associates them with the duke. The Wildonie family reached the apex of its wealth during the lives of Ulrich and Leutold, and the list of their properties, including extensive holdings outside of Styria, is a long one.[2] Leutold died in 1249; Ulrich is last mentioned in 1262 as being in Vienna with his sons among the retinue of King Ottokar of Bohemia.

Extant records say nothing either of the birth or of the mother of the minnesinger Herrand II von Wildonie. His name appears for the first time in a document of 1248, when he was probably in his twenties, and for the last time in 1278. The thirty years between were perhaps the most chaotic and violent in the history of Styria, and Herrand played a leading role in the political affairs of the country throughout the period.

---

[2] Ibid., pp. 230-32.

INTRODUCTION

With the death in 1246 of the last of the Babenbergs, Duke Friedrich II, in a battle against the Hungarians at the Leitha River, Styria became a prize for which its more powerful neighbors struggled until the death of King Ottokar in 1278 enabled Rudolf I of Hapsburg to establish effective and permanent control of the country. The conflict over Styria was one of many in western Europe which resulted from the weakness of the Empire during the imperial interregnum between the end of the Hohenstaufen dynasty, marked by the death of Emperor Friedrich II in 1250, and the rise of the House of Hapsburg with the election of Rudolf I as king of Germany in 1273. Bohemia and Hungary were the major opponents in the struggle for the possession of Styria; the Church and the lesser nobility were secondary forces which shifted their support from one to the other of the chief combatants as was necessary to protect their own interests. It is probable that the lesser nobility could have been the deciding force if it had not been itself divided into Hungarian, Bohemian, Church, and anti-Church factions. Its shifting loyalty was largely a matter of tradition. Perhaps because of their location on the southeast border of the Empire, the knights of Styria had from the time of Charlemagne enjoyed more independence than did the minor nobility in any other German state. The more enlightened knights certainly supported law and order during the tumultuous times, but they were quick to turn against the lawgiver when their traditional privileges became threatened.

From 1246 to 1250 Styria was ruled by two successive imperial governors, but with the death of the emperor his representative gave up this position, leaving the duchy without a head. The members of the Wildonie family were leaders of the pro-Hungarian faction and were able to win over most of the knights to their side, so that in a treaty of 1254 the son of King Béla IV of Hungary became ruler of most of Styria. Herrand apparently still favored Hungary in 1258, for he supported its cause during the fighting over the Salzburg succession which took place that year. As a result of certain misdemeanors the archbishop of Salzburg, Philipp of Carinthia, was deposed by that state's ecclesiastical council, and an ally of King Béla, Archbishop Ulrich of the Styrian diocese of Seckau, was invited to take his place. Philipp, however, had the support of his brother, Duke Ulrich of Carinthia, and his cousin, King Ottokar of Bohemia, and refused to give up his position.

An army of some 500 Styrian knights moved against the Carinthian army at the city of Radstadt, and in the fierce combat that ensued most of the Styrians were killed. Herrand was leading a troop of knights to join in the conflict when he became ill and (fortunately, as it turned out) was obliged to go back alone.[3] It is possible that his sympathies were no longer with King Béla and that he had supported the pro-Hungarian faction in this instance only because of his father-in-law and fellow minnesinger, Ulrich von Liechtenstein, a friend and neighbor of Archbishop Ulrich. Whether Herrand's sickness was the real cause of his retiring before the battle or not, it is clear that he soon lost his Hungarian sympathies because two years later he was with King Ottokar in Vienna and shortly afterward joined other Styrian knights in driving the Hungarians out of the country. His father was the Styrian standard bearer in the battle at Marchfeld in which Béla's forces were decisively defeated.[4]

With the end of Hungarian rule King Ottokar took over control of the country and assumed the title of Duke of Styria. During the first years of his reign Herrand's name appears rather frequently in documents with that of the king or his governor. However, Herrand and many other Styrian nobles gradually became as dissatisfied with Bohemian as they had been with Hungarian domination. A chief point of friction had to do with Ottokar's enforcing a long-neglected law prohibiting the construction by the knights of new fortified positions: walls, towers, or castles. But the tension did not become serious until after the second crusade against the Prussians, which ended abruptly and unsuccessfully. There is no record as to whether Herrand participated in this campaign, but it is not unlikely since his brother-in-law was the commander of the Styrian troops. It was these who suffered the greatest losses during the retreat, and many of them drowned while crossing the Vistula River on thawing ice,

---

[3] An account of the battle and a reference to Herrand's illness is in Chapter 50 of *Ottokars Österreichische Reimchronik,* ed. Josef Seemüller (Hannover, 1890-1893).

[4] The *Reimchronik,* in Chapter 62, refers to the standard bearer merely as "the old Wildoner," without the given name. Friedrich von der Hagen, *Minnesinger: deutsche Liederdichter des 12. 13. und 14. Jahrhunderts,* 5 vols. (Leipzig, 1838-1861), 4:295, assumes that this "old Wildoner" is the minnesinger. Kummer, "Ministerialengeschlecht," p. 239, is probably right in stating that Herrand was still too young to be so designated.

a fact which certainly did not increase the prestige of Ottokar in Styria.

Resolved to forestall an uprising, Ottokar in 1268 summoned Herrand, his brother Hertnid, Ulrich von Liechtenstein, and three other Styrian nobles to Breslau, where they were accused of treason. They were imprisoned in Bohemia and Moravia until their families and relatives turned over the prisoners' castles to the king, who had most of them destroyed. Herrand was held for twenty-six weeks at Eichhorn Castle in Moravia and was freed only when his castles of Eppenstein, Preimarsburg, and Gleichenburg were surrendered to Ottokar's governor. Two were destroyed, but Eppenstein was returned to Herrand intact. [5]

Although subsequent documents show that Herrand continued to cooperate to a certain extent with Ottokar's government, it is clear that the loss of his castles did not endear the Bohemians to him and that he and the other Styrian nobles were ripe for rebellion when Rudolf appeared to challenge Ottokar's right to former Babenberg lands. The rapid decline of Bohemian power at this time certainly was due in part to the activities of Herrand and Hertnid. After Rudolf was elected king of Germany in 1273, Hertnid went to the royal court to urge him to take over Austria and Styria and remained with him as an advisor until the invasion of the two countries had begun. Herrand was one of the Styrian nobles who in 1276 signed a statement renouncing Ottokar and declaring allegiance to Rudolf. With the beginning of hostilities he joined the other nobles in seizing the castles which the Bohemians had occupied and in driving them from the duchy. He had some difficulty in retaking his castle of Eppenstein, which had been occupied by Bohemian troops before the beginning of Rudolf's invasion. However, in the course of the siege he captured seventeen of the enemy and threatened to hang them all if the garrison did not surrender the castle. At this the commander of the Bohemian forces capitulated and was permitted to withdraw. [6]

Little is known of Herrand's private life. He married Perchta, a daughter of Ulrich von Liechtenstein, some time before 1260 and had two sons: Ulrich II, who inherited his title of Lord High

---

[5] This episode is related in Chapters 85 and 86 of the *Reimchronik*.
[6] This episode is related in Chapter 74 of the *Reimchronik*.

Chamberlain, and Herrand III. Herrand III had a daughter, Sophie, who was apparently the last direct descendant of the poet. The other male lines of the house of Wildonie disappeared at about the same time. There are indications of considerable ill feeling between Herrand and his brother during Herrand's last years, for Hertnid was apparently not only quarrelsome but also a wastrel. It may have been his extravagance that diminished the family properties greatly during Herrand's lifetime. A document of 1278 in which the brothers recorded the division of their inheritance shows it to be much smaller than that held by their father and uncle, although the latter had died without a male heir. Herrand's poor health may have brought about the legal assessment and division of property, for there is no record of him after 1278, and he definitely was deceased before 1282.

The Tales

The extant works of Herrand von Wildonie consist of four tales in verse and three minnesongs. Three of the tales appear only in the *Ambraser Heldenbuch,* which Emperor Maximilian I at the beginning of the sixteenth century caused to be prepared from older manuscripts. They are written in Early New High German. A fourth tale of the *Heldenbuch* is included also in a fifteenth-century collection of prose versions of older verse narratives.[7] All of the printed editions of the tales present them in Middle High German translations, which differ considerably. The minnesongs were preserved only in the *Manessische Liederhandschrift* of the early fourteenth century. In this case the manuscript versions are certainly very close to the originals. Herrand is remembered primarily for his narrative verse, perhaps less because it is superior to his songs than because he is one of the very few authors of medieval short stories about whom we have any biographical information and is the only nobleman of his time who is known to have composed in this genre. However that may be, Herrand, although a minor poet of the minnesong, is sometimes ranked second only to Stricker in thirteenth-

---

[7] Michael Curschmann, "Ein neuer Fund zur Überlieferung des Nackten Kaiser von Herrand von Wildonie," *Zeitschrift für deutsche Philologie* 86 (1967): 22-58.

century German literature as a composer of short narrative verse. [8]

Herrand's biographer, Karl Kummer, has attempted to show that Stricker exerted a significant influence on Herrand's tales and that they were noticeably affected by the works of other Middle High German poets, especially Ulrich von Liechtenstein, Hartmann von Aue, and Wolfram von Eschenbach. He has also tried to derive approximate dates of composition by comparing the content of the tales with events of Herrand's time. [9] However, neither literary influence nor dates of composition can be determined, and for the same reason—Herrand's content and language lack distinguishing features, and although his verse tales are better than average, they are fully representative of the mainstream of the medieval short story. What is characteristic of Herrand's works is characteristic of

---

[8] Gustav Ehrismann, in his *Geschichte der deutschen Literatur bis zum Ausgang des Mittelalters. Schlussband* (Munich, 1935), p. 109, speaks of Herrand as follows: "Dieser steierische Minnesänger nimmt nach dem Stricker unter den Verfassern kleineren Erzählungen die nächste, allerdings bei weitem nicht so hervorragende Stelle ein. Seine vier Erzählungen ... sind anmutig erzählt, auch in der künstlerischen Form gut." Alfred Kracher, in an article, "Herrand von Wildonie. Politiker, Novellist und Minnesänger," *Blätter für Heimatkunde* 33 (1959): 44, also praises him: "Die vier Geschichten—wir können sie Versnovellen nennen—sind frisch und launig erzählt, in ihren Stoffen keineswegs originell, aber voll Lust am Fabulieren und weit ansprechender als die meisten anderen Dichtungen der beginnenden Verfallszeit." On the other hand, Karl Kummer, in *Die poetischen Erzählungen des Herrands von Wildonie und die kleinen innerösterreichischen Minnesinger* (Vienna, 1880), p. 55, is much less complimentary: "Es fehlt ihm an origineller Erfindung; er benützt daher alte, bekannte Stoffe zu bestimmten Zwecken und sucht dieselben zu beleben, aber nicht immer glücklich; indem er die Anordnung verändert, verfällt er oft in lästige Wiederholungen.... Die Einleitungsverse sind recht ungeschickt; die Nutzanwendung wird mitunter bei den Haaren herbeigezogen. Reminiscenzen wendet er an, um seine eigene Dürftigkeit zu verhüllen, wo sie sich ihm bieten. Seine Reime bewegen sich in ausgetretenen Geleisen."

[9] Kummer, *Poetische Erzählungen*, pp. 24-34, 47-54. In his review of this work in the *Zeitschrift für die österreichischen Gymnasien* 33 (1882): 215-28, Hans Lambel doubts that Stricker, Hartmann, or Wolfram influenced Herrand significantly and believes that Kummer greatly exaggerates the influence of Ulrich. This doubt is shared by Oswald Zingerle in his review of the same work in the *Anzeiger für deutsches Altertum* 7 (1881): 151-64. Edward Schröder, in "Herrand von Wildon und Ulrich von Liechtenstein," *Nachrichten von der königlichen Gesellschaft der Wissenschaften zu Göttingen* (Berlin, 1924), pp. 33-62, and Kracher both maintain that no literary relationship between Herrand and Stricker can be established. Lambel is also not convinced by Kummer's attempt to date the stories and believes that the order in which they appear in the *Heldenbuch* is not necessarily chronological.

hundreds of other products of the late Middle Ages. It was a period which appreciated artistry in the treatment of traditional material in a traditional form but did not demand originality.

The traditional form which Herrand employed for his tales consists of rhymed couplets in iambic tetrameter, which may be varied by the omission of the initial unaccented syllable, the omission of another unaccented syllable so as to bring two stresses together, the substitution of a dactyl for any of the iambs, or the addition of a final unaccented syllable to make a feminine rhyme. Occasionally trimeter lines occur; they may be altered like tetrameter lines except that trimeter lines which lack the initial unaccented syllable will have a final unstressed syllable. Only rarely do trimeter lines have masculine endings or rhyme with tetrameter lines.

Herrand's meter is more regular than that of most of the narrative poets of his time. He avoids the truncated iambs of his contemporaries by shifting the accent, adding a toneless *e*, drawing out long vowels and diphthongs, or by employing syncope, apocope, or merely a hiatus. He also seldom leaves off the initial unstressed syllable.[10] Herrand uses impure rhyme rather infrequently, resembling in this respect as well as in his employment of fairly regular meter the narrative poets of the early thirteenth century more than his contemporaries.[11] With regard to metrics, the most distinguishing characteristics of Herrand's narrative verse is the rarity of feminine rhyme. Whereas most of his contemporaries used feminine rhyme in 25 to 40 percent of their lines, it occurs in his tales only 5.44 percent of the time.[12]

Of the narrative poets of Herrand's generation only Ulrich von Liechtenstein used feminine rhyme so infrequently, and he only in his long novel, *The Service of Ladies*. It is possible that the metrics of the novel may have influenced those of Herrand's short stories. If so, such influence suggests another basis for dating the composition of the stories, for the first part of one of them, "The Naked Emperor," has a high percentage of feminine rhyme. One might

---

[10] Schröder, p. 37, writes: "Im Streben nach dem Auftakt bleibt er nur wenig hinter Ulrich zurück: auf die 1610 Verse seiner Erzählungen fallen (47 + 78 + 128 + 39 =) 292 ohne solche, d. h. 18,2 %."

[11] Zingerle, in his review of Kummer's *Poetische Erzählungen*, p. 153, states that there are about 100 instances of impure rhyme in Herrand's tales.

[12] Schröder provides data for Herrand and many other thirteenth-century poets

assume that this was Herrand's first tale, that he composed the beginning of it before reading or hearing Ulrich's work, and that he finished it and the other stories before the influence of the novel on his rhyming was dissipated. This reasoning would establish the date of composition of Herrand's verse tales as 1255 or 1256 since *The Service of Ladies* was probably completed in 1255. However, it is certainly possible that the literary influence, if any, could work the other way. Herrand might have begun composing with a high frequency of feminine rhyme, changed for some unknown reason to almost exclusively masculine rhyme, and influenced with this later style the metrics of his father-in-law—a possibility only slightly less plausible than the former.

Herrand's four stories represent four types of medieval verse tales: novella, anecdote, religious legend, and beast fable. The one which appears first in the *Heldenbuch,* the novella, is preceded by a prologue which describes the kind of story the narrator likes to hear. This prologue may be the reason that the tale was placed first, for although two others have prologues, theirs are neither as long nor as general. The novella, entitled "The Faithful Wife," is one of a number of medieval German tales based on the theme of conjugal devotion. It tells of a worthy but most unprepossessing knight who loses an eye in a battle and is ashamed to return to his beautiful wife. To convince him that she loves him and will not be repelled by his disfigurement she takes a pair of scissors and pierces one of her own eyes. There is another, anonymous version of the same story.[13] The chief differences between Herrand's tale and the other have to do with style rather than plot. The former has a more regular meter, is more carefully constructed, and is more sophisticated. It also gives a larger role to the narrator, who has a sense of humor and a tendency toward romantic irony.[14] The fact that Herrand's tale is more polished has led some scholars to assume that the anonymous version is older and that the knight used

---

[13] It is included as "Daz ouge" in Friedrich Heinrich von der Hagen, *Gesamtabenteuer,* 3 vols. (Stuttgart, 1850), 1:245-56.
[14] As in the aside (ll. 75-79):

>und wære er dâ heime beliben,
>so müeset ir iuch hân verzigen,
>daz ich iu niemer het geseit
>von aller siner frümikeit.

Hanns Fischer, ed., *Herrand von Wildonie* (Tübingen, 1959).

it in composing his version.[15] Although this theory is possible, it is not necessarily true, for the medieval verse tales were transmitted primarily by word of mouth, and a popular development of Herrand's story very soon would have lost whatever sophistication it once possessed.

A second literary connection of "The Faithful Wife" is suggested by the lines

> she thought that Absalom could not be
> as fair or Samson strong as he

which appear almost unchanged in Ulrich von Liechtenstein's *Frauenbuch*.[16] But since there are no other important similarities between the two works, the close parallel means no more than that the two poets may have known each other's verse. Some scholars have drawn the conclusion, however, that Herrand's story was composed after 1257, the assumed date of composition of the *Frauenbuch*.[17] This is debatable, for it cannot be established that Ulrich's work was the earlier.

Although the metrics of "The Faithful Wife" are relatively sophisticated, its subject matter shows the hard realism which for the most part is characteristic of the medieval short story. The

---

[15] Schröder, p. 56; Helmut De Boor, *Die deutsche Literatur im späten Mittelalter* (Munich, 1962), p. 248; Kummer, *Poetische Erzählungen*, p. 37. Kummer considers the anonymous version to be superior and criticizes Herrand's story: "In der Wildon'schen Darstellung verraten die Hand des Nachahmers gewisse ausschmückende Zusätze und Steigerungen, welche die dem Dichter abgehende Kraft und Lebendigkeit ersetzen sollen."

[16] Herrand (ll. 49-50):
> er dûhte sî schœne als Absolôn
> und sterker danne Sampsôn.

Ulrich (Lachmann's edition, p. 610, ll. 9-10):
> sî sint schœne als Absolôn
> und sterker danne Sampsôn.

Comparisons involving Absalom and Samson were common in medieval literature, and the similarity of the lines above may be pure coincidence. The fifteenth-century poet Hans Rosenplüt writes:

> Hab dir Sampsons sterck und krafft
> und Allexanders herschafft
> und hab dir die schön Absoloms.

Hermann Maschek, *Lyrik des späten Mittelalters* (Leipzig, 1939), p. 243.

[17] Kummer, *Poetische Erzählungen*, p. 24.

formal minnesong and the courtly novel are set in a wish-land from which ugliness and the seamy side of life have been banned. The short story, however, whether it deals with knights or peasants, the supernatural or the commonplace, generally transpires in the real world in which both knights and peasants live. The difference in tone between the minnesong and courtly novel on the one hand and the short story on the other, therefore, does not indicate a different audience or time (although most short stories were recorded after the classic period of courtly verse) so much as a different genre. In the courtly novel brave knights are not ugly and beautiful ladies do not permanently disfigure themselves, as in "The Faithful Wife," but Herrand is not exceptional in describing such things in the novella.[18] Among other medieval German tales which treat constant love are "Hero and Leander," "Pyramus and Thisbe," and "The Paris Student."

Herrand's second story, "The Deceived Husband," belongs to the most popular type of medieval short story, the amusing anecdote, and its theme is one which was very frequently used in the anecdotes —the unfaithful wife who makes a fool of her husband. We learn of an old knight's young wife who arranges a rendezvous with a lover. So that she can wake up when he comes and steal away from her husband, she ties a string to her toe and drops the loose end

---

[18] De Boor's discussion of Herrand's first two tales stresses their realism but neglects to mention that the *Ritterdichtung* of the short story is not that of the novel (p. 249): "Herrand verlegt beide Erzählungen in das ritterliche Milieu. Aber wie weit sind wir hier von aller Ritterdichtung entfernt! Der Hässliche als Held einer Geschichte, die Selbstzerstörung von Frauenschönheit als preisenwerte Tat bis hinab zu dem unhöfischen Instrument, mit dem sie geschieht, der Schere, liegen jenseits aller Möglichkeiten höfischen Erzählens. Inneren Adel zu preisen ist auch das Anliegen des höfischen Dichters, aber es hätte ihn gegraust, diesen an einer so handgreiflichen Tat demonstrieren zu sollen. Auch der höfische Dichter lässt die Frau in der Emphase des Schmerzes sich entstellen, die Haare ausraufen, die Brüste zerschlagen, die Wangen zerkratzen. Aber es bleiben die vorgeschriebenen Gebärden, und niemals wird er die Narben sehen, die davon zurückbleiben. Die ganz unemphatische Opfertat dieser Frau entstellt sie fürs Leben, und gerade darin liegt ihre Grösse. Die Liebe, die sie dazu befähigt, entspringt aus anderen Quellen als die höfische Minne; sie ist höchste Bewährung der Treue in der Wirklichkeit des Alltags, vor der die höfische Welt der Schönheit verblasst." Michael Curschmann, however, in his article "Zur literarhistorischen Stellung Herrands von Wildonie," *Deutsche Vierteljahresschrift für Literaturwissenschaft und Geistesgeschichte* 40 (1966): 56-79, emphasizes the courtly nature of Herrand's tale.

down from the oriel where they sleep. The lover comes and pulls the string, but it is the husband who awakes. He hurries down and seizes the intruder. His wife follows and offers to hold the lover while the husband goes to bring a light. When he returns she is holding a donkey which, she swears, was what was turned over to her. The angry husband goes back to bed, but the wife persuades a friend to take her place in the bedroom. Thinking the woman to be his wife, the old knight beats her and cuts off her hair. When he goes to sleep the woman departs, taking her hair, and the wife returns to her husband. The next morning she convinces him by her long hair and absence of bruises that he has imagined the entire occurrence.

This story appears in various forms in many literatures. It has been suggested that the oldest extant version is the second tale of the Sanskrit *Baital-Pachisi*. In the best-known version of the Sanskrit anecdote the wife steals out to her lover, who has been murdered by a robber while he waits for her. Thinking him asleep, she bends over to kiss him and has the end of her nose bitten off by the corpse, which has been taken over momentarily by a demon. To conceal her shame she goes back to the house, cries loudly, and makes the assembled neighbors believe that her husband has cut off her nose. [19]

There is a closer parallel to Herrand's tale in a narrative from another Sanskrit collection, the famous *Panchatantra*, which has the same plot employed by the Austrian knight. In it a drunken weaver suspects his wife of infidelity, ties her up, and falls asleep. The barber's wife unties her and takes her place while she goes to see her lover. The husband wakes up and speaks to the bound woman. When she will not answer, he cuts off her nose and falls asleep again. When his wife returns she unbinds her friend, resumes her former place, and calls loudly on the gods to make her nose grow out again as a proof that she is a virtuous woman. When the husband sees the undamaged nose, he is filled with regret because of his violent deed and apparently unfounded suspicions. [20]

---

[19] Richard F. Burton, trans., *Vikram and the Vampire* (London, 1893), pp. 92-102.

[20] Arthur W. Ryder, trans., *The Panchatantra* (Chicago, 1925), pp. 62-71.

INTRODUCTION 21

All the essential elements of Herrand's narrative are here except the string and the animal. The latter appears in the oldest extant European version of the tale, that by the French poet Guerin. He tells how the husband catches the lover in the house at night and, believing him a thief, lets his wife hold him while he gets a light and his sword. During his absence she substitutes a mule for the lover, whch so angers the husband when he returns that he orders her from the house. A servant woman takes her place, and the man, thinking his wife has returned, beats the maid and cuts off her hair. The wife then goes back to her husband, who is now asleep, removes the hair from beneath his pillow, and puts there a horse's tail. The next morning she convinces him that the experiences of the night were a hallucination. [21]

Many other variants of the story appeared during the Middle Ages, the most famous being the eighth tale of the seventh day in Boccaccio's *Decameron*. A woman ties a string to her toe so that her lover may awaken her. Her husband notices the string while she is asleep, removes it, ties it to his own toe, and is soon awakened by the lover. He seizes a sword and pursues the man who, after a fight, makes his escape. The wife induces a maid to take her place in the bed, extinguishes the light, and hides. When the husband returns, he beats the maid, cuts off her hair, and goes to bring the wife's relatives to witness to the fact that he is justified in driving her away. When they arrive and find that she has not been beaten, has lost no hair, and that the bed apparently has not been slept in,

---

[21] Etienne Barbazan, ed., *Fabliaux et Contes des XIe, XIIe, XIIIe, XIVe, et XVe Siècles*, 4 vols. (Paris, 1808), 4:393-407. Hans Lambel, in *Erzählungen und Schwänke* (Leipzig, 1872), p. 208, and Paul Piper, in *Höfische Epik*, 3 vols. (Stuttgart, 1892-1895), 3:412, name the *Baital-Pachisi* story as the earliest version of the tale. They cite the account in the *Panchatantra* as a second step in its development. Friedrich von der Hagen (*Gesamtabenteuer*, 2:xlii) begins with the latter work. Joseph Bédier, however, in *Les Fabliaux* (Paris, 1895), pp. 164-200, asserts that one cannot derive the tale of Guerin directly from any Oriental source and that the early French story, although perhaps indirectly influenced by that in the *Panchatantra*, was essentially a Western product. He points out that the Latin translation which introduced the *Panchatantra* to western Europe was not made until the latter part of the thirteenth century. Most contemporary scholars follow Bédier in tending to be skeptical about Oriental sources for the European verse tale, although the possibility of an Eastern influence being exerted through Moorish Spain and the Arabic *Kalila wa-Dimna* is recognized.

they turn on the husband and threaten him so severely that he never again dares cross his wife. From then on she can do without fear anything she wishes. [22]

The last important medieval version of the tale, the sixty-first of the *Cent Nouvelles Nouvelles,* was probably directly influenced by Boccaccio. In it a merchant becomes suspicious of his wife and, having pretended to leave the vicinity, watches his house from that of a neighbor. Seeing a knight loitering before the dwelling, the merchant pretends to be a servant, leads him into the house, and locks him in a room. He then goes to collect his wife's relatives so that they may witness her shame. The wife, however, discovers what has happened, frees her lover, and puts a donkey in his place. When the relatives arrive to punish the wife and kill the captured knight they are greeted by the loud braying of the donkey. They would have killed the merchant had he not taken flight. Afterward he always did just as his wife desired. [23] In this late variant one can see how the anonymous author selected from among the various elements of the tale. He used the relatives and the substitution of donkey for lover but discarded the string and the substitution of one woman for another. It is a good story and does not suffer from its economy of motifs.

Herrand's story is one of two Middle High German representatives of this tale. The other, "The Priest with the String," has all the basic elements of "The Deceived Husband" as well as Boccaccio's scene involving the neighbors and relatives. In this anonymous version the relatives, believing the husband insane, drag him off to the priest (his wife's lover), who tries to drive out the evil spirit with a mass. When the husband persists in claiming to be sane, holes are burned in his head with incense. At last he is convinced that he has been mad. [24]

There are more Middle High German stories which employ some of the motifs of Herrand's work. The substitution of one woman for another takes place in "Two Merchants and the Faithful

---

[22] Richard Aldington, trans., *The Decameron of Giovanni Boccaccio* (Garden City, N.Y., 1930), pp. 377-83.
[23] Thomas Wright, ed., *Les Cent Nouvelles Nouvelles,* 2 vols. (Paris, 1857), 2:53-60.
[24] Heinrich Niewöhner, ed., *Neues Gesamtabenteuer* (Berlin, 1937), pp. 89-96. There are three variants of this tale.

INTRODUCTION   23

Wife" and "The Heron"; [25] in "The Nussberg" a prisoner is freed by the wife of the knight who captured him; [26] in "The Substituted Calf" an animal replaces a lover. [27] We do not know Herrand's source. At the beginning of his tale he claims to have heard it from Ulrich von Liechtenstein, whom he cites as a witness to its truth. Ulrich was famous for a fantastic, slapstick novel which he asserted to be completely factual; thus Herrand's use of him to establish the truth of a story immediately sets the stage for comedy. In a later century he would have cited Baron Münchhausen. Since the reference to Ulrich speaks of him as living, the story must have been composed before 1275, the year of Ulrich's death. Although in general medieval anecdotes rely heavily on erotic elements for their interest, Herrand's treatment of the cuckold theme is typical in that it stresses the cleverness of the wife rather than the act of adultery. [28]

An equally popular subject is treated in Herrand's religious legend, "The Naked Emperor." It tells of a haughty Roman emperor named Gorneus who becomes enraged by a passage in the Gospel according to Luke which promises that the proud and mighty shall be abased. [29] He declares that the Scriptures lie, stops attending mass, and makes no further attempt to rule wisely. After ten years, however, he announces that he will hold court and invites all who have suffered injustice to come to Rome and be heard. The night before the beginning of the court session, while Gorneus is at the bath-house, an angel assumes his form, dons his clothes, and rides away with the emperor's retinue. Gorneus is taken for an imposter and driven out naked, save for some twigs which give him scanty covering. He can find no one who will believe that he is the emperor. The judgment day arrives, and the angel dispenses such justice that

---

[25] Hagen, *Gesamtabenteuer*, 3:351-83; 2:153-71.
[26] Ibid., 1:441-49.
[27] Hanns Fischer, ed., *Die deutsche Märendichtung des 15. Jahrhunderts* (Munich, 1966), pp. 294-99.
[28] Hanns Fischer, *Studien zur deutschen Märendichtung* (Tübingen, 1968), pp. 102-3: "Gegenüber dieser intellektuell bestimmten Handlungskomik, die solchermassen als die zentrale Komik der Märendichtung anzusehen ist, erweist sich das erotische Element aufs Ganze gesehen als akzessorisch."
[29] Several verses would be appropriate, but the most likely one is Luke 14:11: "For whosoever exalteth himself shall be abased; and he that humbleth himself shall be exalted."

many of the rich and mighty are beheaded and the poor receive their due. At last Gorneus repents of his pride and the neglect of his duties and the angel gives him back his clothing and his position. From then on the emperor rules justly and honors God.

Herrand combines two themes which were frequently treated in medieval literature: the haughty ruler who loses his identity along with his clothing while taking a bath and the severe but righteous judgment which a monarch visits on those who misuse their power. [30] Although various Oriental narratives, including the Biblical story of Nebuchadnezzar, treat similar themes, there is none which resembles Herrand's to the extent that one might assume a literary influence. However, many medieval legends of western Europe are obviously closely related to "The Naked Emperor." The closest resemblance is in the German story, "The King in the Bath," which tells of the fall and restoration of a monarch but omits the wholesale executions of the plundering nobles. The similarity between the two works is such that it is quite likely either that one directly influenced the other or that both drew from the same immediate source. [31] "The King in the Bath" has more rough comedy than Herrand's version and, since the whole plot turns about the king's denial of God's power to abase the mighty, it is more unified. However, it is cruder and not as well told as "The Naked Emperor."

Another, later version of the story is in the *Gesta Romanorum,* a collection of tales in Latin which was made probably about the

---

[30] Curschmann, "Zur literarhistorischen Stellung Herrands von Wildonie," p. 64, interprets Herrand's legend as having a sociological rather than a theological moral: "Bei ihm handelt es sich nicht um die Geschichte des Mächtigen, der glaubt, *daz nieman möhte ob im sin* ('König im Bade' 15), und in einem jähen Fall die Grenzen seiner Macht erkennen muss; er erzählt die Geschichte des Herrschers, der in seiner Selbstüberschätzung nur Rechte für sich in Anspruch nimmt, deshalb seine Herrscherpflichten vernachlässigt und durch Selbsterkenntnis in die Grenzen seines Amtes zurückfindet.... Die Selbstüberhebung des Kaisers besteht in Pflichtvergessenheit, die Missachtung des biblischen Satzes ist eher Symptom als Akt des Hochmuts."

[31] Kummer, *Poetische Erzählungen,* assumes that "The King in the Bath" was by Herrand's older contemporary, Stricker, and that Herrand's tale drew directly from this work. However, Lambel, in his review of Kummer's book, denies both that Stricker was the author of "The King in the Bath" and that Herrand was necessarily acquainted with the story. Schröder agrees with Lambel with regard to the authorship of "The King in the Bath" and believes that Herrand's work is the older of the two. He thinks that the two stories have a common source.

end of the thirteenth century. In it an emperor named Jovianus believes himself to be God. He bathes while hunting and loses clothing and identity to an angel who takes the emperor's place while Jovianus is repudiated and beaten. When the emperor confesses and repents of his excessive pride, he is restored to his previous position. Unlike "The King in the Bath," the Latin story does not exploit the comic potential of the situation and concentrates specifically on the moral. It resembles in various details both of the previous tales, even where they do not resemble each other. Once more the judgment and punishment of the evildoers is left out. [32] In the fourteenth century a German translation of the *Gesta Romanorum* appeared which later supplied Hans Sachs with many themes for plays and tales. Hans Sachs retells the Jovianus story in a "Comedia, mit 9 personen zu agiern: Julianus, der kayser, im badt und hat 5 actus" [33] and in a narrative poem, "Der hoffertig kaiser Aurelianus in dem pad." [34] Although Hans Sachs alters his material freely, even to twice changing the name of the central figure, he follows the *Gesta* version (to which he refers) in all significant features.

Other treatments of this material are found in a narrative poem by the fifteenth-century German writer Hans Rosenplüt; a *Meistergesang*; an English morality play, "Robert Cycyl"; and a play by the seventeenth-century Spanish dramatist Rodrigo de Herrera. [35]

Perhaps the best-known version of the tale is the fourteenth-century English poem "Robert of Sicily." In it appears the passage from Luke, but the angel takes the king's place in church rather than while he is bathing. After having vainly attempted to establish his identity, King Robert becomes the court fool and remains so for more than three years. At last he repents of his pride and is restored to his former position. In two respects this variant follows that of Herrand and differs from "The King in the Bath" and the Latin poem: King Robert regains his position without the court's learning (until after his death) of the angel's existence, and there is

---

[32] Charles Swan, trans., *Gesta Romanorum* (London, n.d.), pp. 159-65.
[33] A. v. Keller and E. Goetze, eds., *Hans Sachs*, 26 vols. (Tübingen, 1870-1908), 13:110-41.
[34] Ibid., 22:505-7.
[35] Hagen, *Gesamtabenteuer*, 3:cxv-cxx.

mention of the fact that the angel brought justice and harmony to the land.[36]

Even though "Robert of Sicily" adds the idea of the just ruler to the central theme of the mighty being brought low, it does not develop this idea into a significant motif. And since the other well-known treatments of the theme do not deal with royal or imperial justice at all, some literary historians have attempted to connect this part of "The Naked Emperor" with political events of Herrand's time. However, there are Middle High German narratives which tell of the severe judgment which a new ruler executes on those who misuse their power. The author of "Kudrun" reports that when Hagen became king of Ireland he had more than eighty nobles decapitated because of their depredations. In the same connection the author speaks of the hardship to the poor which is caused by the burning of villages, a deed which Herrand's angel-emperor punishes with death.

Another, closer parallel to the trial and judgment scenes of "The Naked Emperor" is found in the verse tale "Emperor Dagobert," which is also in other respects like Herrand's story. Once when the imperial throne was to be filled the cardinals and princes gathered to choose an emperor. They all had the same revelation: the emperor would be called Dagobert, and he would be a poor and righteous man who, when on the throne, would establish peace and justice. The one they sought turned out to be an egg merchant who was so poor that he had to carry his merchandise on his back. He was found by some boys and brought against his will to Rome. At first Dagobert believed that he was being ridiculed by those who said he was to be emperor and begged to be left alone. He also asked for food since he had not eaten in three days. Once crowned, he was a strong ruler, and when many of the nobles refused to cease their robbery and arson, he seized them and had them beheaded. From that time on none dared to oppose his authority, and peace prevailed throughout the empire.[37] Besides the holding of court and the executions, these incidents recall Herrand's narrative: Gorneus

---

[36] Walter French and Charles Hale, eds., *Middle English Metrical Romances* (New York, 1930), pp. 931-46. This work inspired the poem by Edward Rowland Sill, "The Fool's Prayer," which was at one time very popular.

[37] Hagen, *Gesamtabenteuer*, 2:563-75.

insists that he is emperor and the people make fun of him, while Dagobert does not believe that he is to be emperor and thinks that people are making fun of him; Gorneus has to work with boys in the kitchen to get food, while Dagobert is brought to Rome by boys and there asks for food; a porter gives Gorneus an old coat to hide his nakedness, while the boys put a fishing net over Dagobert.

The historical events which have been mentioned as source material for Herrand's story are related to Gorneus's exploitation: depreciation and manipulation of currency to his advantage, excessive taxation, and the seizing of fiefs whenever the right of succession was in any doubt. Although complaints of the minor nobility against such activities on the part of the ruling princes are recorded throughout the Middle Ages and in all the German lands, it is thought by some that resentment was particularly strong in Styria and especially during the period from the death of Emperor Friedrich II in 1250 to 1260, when the duchy threw off Hungarian rule and accepted that of Ottokar.[38] During the early part of this decade Ottokar had seized Styria but had been driven out when most of the knights joined forces with the Hungarians. He won their support in 1259 by promising to preserve carefully all their hereditary privileges. If these occurrences have a bearing on Herrand's story, which is somewhat doubtful, it means that Ottokar served as the model for Gorneus. It is interesting in this connection to note that the period of lawlessness described in the tale lasted just ten years.

Another possible source for Herrand's story is one which the author mentions in his opening lines, a German prose manuscript. Such a document, if it really existed, would have been most unusual, for prose was ordinarily written in Latin. If the manuscript was merely invented by the author, the reason is not difficult to see: prose was more factual than verse and would lend authenticity to his tale. That he should invent a German rather than a Latin source

---

[38] Joseph Bergmann, in "Des steyermärkischen Herrn und Sängers Herant von Wildon vier poetische Erzählungen aus der Mitte des dreyzehnten Jahrhunderts," *Anzeige-Blatt für Wissenschaft und Kunst* 95 (1841): 49, cites a number of historical sources which refer to the discontent of the minor nobility in Styria because of currency manipulation. Kummer, in *Poetische Erzählungen,* p. 29, and Piper, in *Höfische Epik,* 3:414, discuss contemporary events which, they believe, influenced the story.

may have been because he did not think that he, a knight, could make a plausible claim to knowing Latin.[39]

Whatever Herrand's immediate source or sources may have been, it is certain that the tale in one form or another was widely known in the thirteenth century.[40] Perhaps Wolfram von Eschenbach was referring to it in *Parzival* when he said that sooner than have people think he was composing a book he would sit naked in a bath without a towel. Of course, he continued, he wouldn't forget his bundle of twigs.[41]

The last of Herrand's tales as they appear in the Ambraser Manuscript, the beast fable entitled "The Cat," treats a story which appeared in many forms during the Middle Ages and has been used by several modern authors. A tomcat is so egotistical that he feels much superior to his wife and desires to have the mightiest female in all creation for a mate. He therefore leaves his lowly companion and journeys to the sun, to whom he proposes marriage. When the sun discovers why the tomcat has chosen her, she sends him on to the fog who, she says, is strong enough to hide her most powerful rays. The fog in turn sends him to the wind, who can drive her away at will; the wind refers him to the wall, who has withstood the stormiest blasts of the wind for a century; the wall tells the

---

[39] Schröder accepts Herrand's statement concerning a German prose source and says (p. 55): "Damit gewinnen wir für die Geschichte der erzählenden deutschen Prosa in mhd. Zeit wieder ein wertvolles Zeugnis, das nach der Auffindung von frühen Fragmenten des Prosa-Lanzelet nicht mehr anstössig wirken kann, und zugleich haben wir einen freilich zunächst kaum verwertbaren Hinweis auf die bisher noch völlig unaufgeklärte Vorgeschichte eben der 'Gesta Romanorum.' "

[40] It is not surprising that the Middle Ages, with their strong caste system, should have been intrigued by the literary possibilities of a complete reversal of a man's position in the system. The compatibility of this theme with the times has been demonstrated in many pieces of modern fiction set in the Middle Ages, such as Twain's *The Prince and the Pauper*.

[41] The last lines of Book 2 read:

> ê man si hete vür ein buoch,
> ich wære ê nacket âne tuoch
> sô ich in dem bade sæze,
> ob ich squesten niht vergæze.

The helplessness of a man in a bathtub and the potential for embarrassment were frequently exploited for comic purposes by medieval writers. Wolfram, Gottfried von Strassburg, and Ulrich von Liechtenstein, among others, describe humorous bathtub scenes. So does Walther von der Vogelweide, but in this case the occupant of the tub was a lady.

cat of a mouse who has made so many holes in her that she may fall at any moment; the mouse is afraid of him because he so much resembles her terrible mistress, the female cat. So the hero returns to his wife and, after being thoroughly scolded, resumes his former marital position, a wiser and humbler tomcat. To the story Herrand attaches a somewhat lengthy moral: men ought to remain with the lords of their youth and not go off seeking new ones.

The same fable is treated somewhat differently by Stricker. Here the tomcat is just as proud of himself but has no mate. He goes to a vixen to seek her aid in finding a wife who can compare with him in splendor. She suggests in turn the daughters of the sun, the fog, the wind, the stone house, the mouse, and the cat, showing the superiority of each prospect over the preceding one. When the vixen comes to the end of the list, she severely admonishes the tomcat for his excessive pride. Finally the author gives the appropriate warning against a too haughty spirit. In that it is the daughters of the various phenomena whom Stricker brings forth as possible brides, his version avoids the awkwardness that appears in Herrand's story because of the grammatically masculine fog and wind.[42] Although the plots of the two variants are quite similar, a comparison of language and rhyme does not indicate a specific influence of one on the other.[43]

A resemblance to Herrand's tale which in some ways is closer than Stricker's narrative can be seen in a tale by the early fourteenth-century Jewish writer, Rabbi Berachja Hanakdan.[44] Although the hero of the Hebrew version is a mouse, in other respects the story follows that of Herrand. One after the other the mouse woos the sun, the cloud, the wind, and the wall before he becomes humble and takes a wife of his own kind. Although no epilogue is attached to the story, the moral is in general the same as in "The Cat." In a Middle Low German version of the tale the mouse, through a scribal

---

[42] Ute Schwab, ed., *Der Stricker. Tierbispel* (Tübingen, 1966), pp. 41-48.

[43] Piper, p. 418, calls Herrand's story an imitation of Stricker's. Schröder, p. 57, maintains that no literary connection between the two can be established. Curschmann, "Zur literarhistorischen Stellung Herrands von Wildonie," pp. 66-69, compares the two works with regard to the treatment of the main theme.

[44] Lessing translates the story in his "Briefe, die neueste Literatur betreffend," *Gesammelte Werke*, 10 vols. (Berlin, 1954-1957), 4:153-54.

error or a poor translation, has become a mule, which gives an amusing twist to the search for a bride.[45]

The error in transcription or translation may well have been caused by an inconsistency which appeared in the tale during its development. The earliest extant version is that related in the third book of the *Panchatantra*. Here it is a story of a female mouse who picks out a husband. A holy man changes an infant mouse into a baby girl and raises her to the age of twelve, at which time he summons in turn sun, cloud, wind, mountain, and mouse before him in order that his adopted daughter may choose the greatest being as her husband. Each potential suitor defers to the next as the greater and when at last the male mouse comes before the girl she immediately falls in love with him and begs to be transformed into a mouse so that she may wed him; the holy man changes her back to a mouse. The point of the fable is the philosophical idea that like is drawn to like, and the technique is a consistent reversal of values so that what seems to be the least is the greatest.

When the story first appears in a western European language, in the fable collection of Marie de France, two important changes have taken place: it is now a male mouse who seeks a wife, and the dominant idea is moral rather than philosophical. The story now teaches humility, telling how the ambitious and presumptuous male mouse is at last led to wed his own kind. A tower is substituted for the mountain, but the reversal of values remains consistent. One thing, however, is wrong with the tale in its altered form. Whereas tiny, timid mice made a logical hero and heroine for the *Panchatantra* story, a mouse is not a convincing hero for an account of overweening pride. The High German versions changed the main character to a haughty tomcat, a suitable casting but one which impairs the consistency of the reversal of values. The Low German translator apparently would not believe that the French *mulez* could mean mouse and so translated it to *mul* (mule), a more likely representative of pride.

"The Wartburg War," an early fourteenth-century narrative, contains a reference to the High German tale which implies that the

---

[45] Bernd Kratz, "Maulesel und Maus auf der Suche nach einer Braut," *Jahrbuch des Vereins für niederdeutsche Sprachforschung* 140 (1968): 87-92.

tale was widely known. Biterolf, one of the participants in a singers' contest, says: "A tomcat thought himself so fine that he wished to wed the sun, just as it rose in the early morning; and yet he later took, after his own kind, an animal which caught mice." [46] It is interesting that Biterolf's reference follows the Hebrew version rather than the other German ones in that the wooing of the sun takes place in the early morning.

If one compares Herrand's story with those of Stricker and Berachja, one notices especially that Herrand's development of the moral is by far the most specific. His warning against continually changing masters has raised the question as to whether Herrand had in mind particular political events of his day, perhaps the wavering of the Styrian nobility between Hungary and Bohemia during the late 1250s. [47]

The Songs

Under the name "Der von Wildonie" in the *Manessische Liederhandschrift* is a picture of two knights dressed for hunting and carrying swords and crossbows. They are riding beneath the castle window of a lady to whom one of the knights is handing a manuscript, perhaps of his verse. Three minnesongs of three stanzas each follow the illustration. That the knight with the manuscript is the Herrand von Wildonie of the verse tales has been generally accepted, but the limited amount of lyric verse by Herrand and its quite traditional style make definite identification impossible. [48] There are some differences in metrics between the stories and the songs, but these are related more to the characteristics of the genres than to those of the poet. For example, in the tales there are twenty-eight instances of apocope in the rhyme, whereas in the songs there are

---

[46]   ein kater dûhte sich sô zart,
    daz er die sunnen wollte vrîen, sô sie vrüeje ûf gienc,
    unde nam doch sint nâch sîner rehten art
    ein tier, daz miuse vienc.

T. A. Rompelman, *Der Wartburgkrieg* (Amsterdam, 1939), p. 158.

[47] Kummer, *Poetische Erzählungen*, p. 27.

[48] In this respect one can scarcely go further than Kummer's statement, ibid., p. 20: "Mit den metrischen Eigentümlichkeiten der Erzählungen Herrands von Wildon steht die Metrik der drei einem Wildoner zugeschriebenen Lieder ... nicht in Widerspruch."

none.[49] However, other Middle High German authors of narrative verse and courtly songs also took such liberties in the former which they would not permit themselves in the latter. Everything considered, it is easier to believe that the knight in the picture is our storyteller than to suppose that there were two poets in the family. Perhaps the other hunter is Herrand's brother, Hertnid.

The poet probably composed much more lyric verse than appears in the Manesse Collection. The condition of the manuscript itself indicates that the scribe left space for more of Herrand's songs, which for some reason he was unable to secure.[50] In addition, a younger colleague, Hugo von Trimberg, lists Herrand among the most famous of the minnesingers, and it is certain that such a reputation must have been based on a larger quantity of lyric verse than is extant.[51] Indeed, it is not likely that any of his songs would have been included in the Manesse Collection had he not been fairly prolific.

In content and form Herrand is quite traditional. All three songs are poems of the seasons and, according to convention, are introduced by descriptions of nature: the first by a winter scene, the other two by May scenes, with flowers, green meadows, leafy forests,

---

[49] Schröder, pp. 38-42, compares in detail the language of the tales and the songs.

[50] Kummer, *Poetische Erzählungen,* pp. 123-24: "Zwischen Brennenberg und Wildonie liegen 10 Blätter (5 Doppelblätter), welche die späteren Nachträge n. 62-65 enthalten. Dass zu Nachträgen für Wildonie und Suneck ausser dem Ueberschuss an leerem Raume auf Spalte 201d und 203b noch je eine Seite offen gehalten wurde, bestätigt die oben ausgesprochene Vermutung, dass von diesen Dichtern ausser den erhaltenen noch andere Lieder bekannt waren, wenn auch der Redactor von C derselben nicht habhaft werden konnte."

[51]
   Gîtikeit, luoder und unkiusche,
   muotwille und unzimlich getiusche
   hânt mangen herren alsô besezzen,
   daz si der wîse gar hânt vergezzen,
   in der hie vor edel herren sungen,
   von Botenloube und von Môrungen,
   von Linburc und von Windesbecke,
   von Nîf, Wildonje und von Brûnecke.
   her Walther von der Vogelweide,
   swer des vergæze, der tæt mir leide:
   aleine er wære niht rich des guotes,
   doch war er sinniges muotes.

Ferdinand Vetter, ed., *Lehrhafte Litteratur des 14. und 15. Jahrhunderts* (Berlin, n.d.), pt. 1, p. 256, ll. 1210-21.

and singing birds. All these signs of spring are part of the standard symbolical language of the minnesong, and although one scholar speaks of Herrand's strong feeling for nature,[52] it must be admitted that he introduces no element of nature into his songs which had not been used previously in a similar manner hundreds of times. Nature introductions for minnesongs were prevalent throughout the thirteenth century, probably because of the great popularity of the verse of Neidhart von Reuenthal. It is likely that most songs of the seasons were dance songs.

The winter scene of the first song is described, in the customary manner, in negative terms as we are told of the absence of flowers and the unhappiness of the birds. This establishes the melancholy mood which characterizes the winter song in general. In the second stanza the narrator declares that the cruel winter shall not keep him from spreading joy with his songs, although he admits that he could do this better if the pangs of love did not afflict him so. Proceeding from his personal experience, he goes on in the third stanza to praise all who value virtue and honor (of which love's suffering is a part) and all who are faithful in love. The progression is simple and direct: from the sadness of winter to the sadness of the narrator to sad lovers everywhere. It is a favorite formula of minnesong composers, but not as common as its variant form: mood of the season to mood of lovers in general to mood or experience of the narrator.

The metrics of the poem are also quite simple, especially for a generation which for the most part took great pride in technical virtuosity. Each stanza is made up of two short *Stollen* with pentameter lines rhyming *a b a b,* and an *Abgesang* consisting of a tetrameter line and a heptameter line which rhyme *c c.* The rhythm is trochaic with occasional dactyls. The three-stanza song, the six-line stanza, the rhythm, and the rhyme scheme all belong to the more popular structural characteristics of the thirteenth-century minnesong and are just as conventional as the content. Yet the song

---

[52] Kracher, p. 52: "Ein starkes Naturgefühl zeichnet alle drei Gedichte aus, das vielfach über die Konvention hinausgeht. In keinem fehlen die Vögel, wenn sie auch im ersten, einem Winterliede, nur zur Verstärkung der traurigen Stimmung dienen ... Heide, Wald, Au, die Rose in Tau, die hellen Sommertage, die strahlende Sonne und vieles ähnliches sind in den insgesamt neun Strophen so gehäuft, wie bei kaum einem anderen mittelhochdeutschen Dichter."

does not sound hackneyed. It has a light grace, a sprightly air for all its would-be sadness, and language which is melodic and natural.

In the first stanza of the second song the singer describes the beauties of May, which cause the birds to rejoice just as he rejoices over the charms of his lady. In the second stanza he calls on sweet love to make the lady respond to his affection and drive away all his care. The last stanza is devoted to praise of the lady and a description of her wondrous beauty. The progression here is also simple and traditional, but a little less so than that of the preceding song: the beauty of nature and the joy of the birds, to the joy of the singer if the lady responded, to the beauty of the lady. The singer is equated with the birds and the lady with May (not uncommon conceits), and the personal reflections once more appear in the middle stanza rather than, as was more common, at the end. The mood, in keeping with the season, is light and gay.

The structure and metrics of the second song are a little more involved than those of the first but are by no means as complicated as those of many of Herrand's contemporaries. There are two three-line *Stollen* with tetrameter, dimeter, and heptameter lines rhyming *a b c a b c*, and a four-line *Abgesang* consisting of three successive tetrameter lines followed by a trimeter line. The *Abgesang* rhymes *d e e d*. The rhythm is basically iambic, but the *Auftakt* is missing for the third line of the *Stollen*.

In the first stanza of the third song the singer proclaims that everyone should be happy because of the splendors of May. At the end of the stanza he hears the birds singing in the forest glades. In the second stanza we learn that the rising sun fills everyone with joy; the singer asks what is so fair as a dew-covered rose and answers: only a kind and beautiful lady. The third stanza declares that love rises in the eyes and enters the heart, where love asks love: when can I come to you? This, we are told, is the song sung by a forest bird.

This last poem has more components than the others, and the transitions are not as smooth. The basic progression is from the universal joy of a spring morning to the comparison of an object of nature with a beautiful lady, to love that ever seeks for love. Again we have a pattern which, with many variations, is frequently seen in the minnesong. In spite of, or perhaps because of, the abrupt jumping from one topic to another, this song makes the strongest impression of the three.

The structure of the third song resembles that of the first in that it has *Stollen,* trochaic rhythm, and the same rhyme scheme. The lines are tetrameter except for the last line, which has eight feet. The last stanza contains an interesting alteration. At some time during the seventy-five or eighty years between its composition and its recording in the Manesse Collection the fifth line disappeared, and someone compensated for it by changing the last line to rhyme with lines two and four, so that the last stanza rhymes *a b a b b.* The result is that the loss of the fifth line is noticed only when the last stanza is compared with the first two.

Herrand brought nothing new to the minnesong. His content is restricted to traditionally poetic objects of nature, a beautiful but nebulous lady, and his love for her. His metrics are equally conventional, the most unusual feature being that all the stanzas end in a line of a different length from that of the others. His style is somewhat more distinctive than his content and form, being marked by rhetorical questions, exclamations, and a tendency to generalize on an experience.[53] His lyric verse is light and pleasing. All that he said had been said before, and in a similar manner, but seldom had it been said better.

Several influences by older poets on Herrand's lyric verse have been mentioned, but we have so little of it and it is so traditional that the enumeration of parallel expressions and constructions is not very meaningful. Where Herrand resembles one poet, he resembles a dozen. Discussions of his influence on other poets are equally inconclusive.[54]

The most prominent characteristic of Herrand's writings is a conservative decorum and a didacticism which are more pronounced than in most similar works by his contemporaries. "The Faithful Wife" is introduced by an expression of regret that so few stories are told in which virtue is stressed; "The Naked Emperor" ends not only with a description of the regeneration of the hero but also

---

[53] Kummer, *Poetische Erzählungen,* pp. 88-89, discusses details of style.
[54] Walther von der Vogelweide, Gottfried von Neifen, and Ulrich von Liechtenstein have been cited most frequently as possible influences on Herrand. Kummer, *ibid.,* pp. 101-2, points out possible influences of Herrand on Otto zem Turne, Brunwart von Augheim, and Konrad von Landeck.

with a prayer that the poet himself may benefit by the tale and that Christ may take away his sins; "The Cat" concludes with a lengthy warning to those who would risk their security (and endanger the social system) by changing masters. Although "The Deceived Husband" contains no lesson or moral, it is almost alone among the many humorous anecdotes of adultery in that the act itself is glossed over in a single, very circumspect line. It is also unusual that Song 1, which because of its nature introduction would appear to be a dance song, ends on a didactic note when one would expect the praise of a beautiful lady or (since it is a winter song) an expression of sorrow over disappointed love.

Neither as a narrative nor as a lyric poet was Herrand an innovator. He not only used the subjects, motifs, and techniques of others, but he even seems to have preferred well-known to novel material. However, to twentieth-century readers originality is perhaps of less importance in a medieval work than is the poet's treatment of what was typical of his time. Herrand's works treat popular themes, but they do so in the careful and well-polished form of the artist. His tales are excellent examples of four of the most prevalent types of short narratives; his songs are charming representatives of the most popular kind of courtly verse. Both are sufficiently simple in style and universal in theme to provide entertainment for any age.

THE TALES

The Faithful Wife
(Diu getriu kone)

We ought to tell of pleasant things
and never dwell on that which brings
unhappiness to those who hear.
Indeed I've wasted many a year
with gloomy stories since a boy 5
which left me oft bereft of joy.
Good stories make one glad, but O
the other kind have irked me so
I do without them willingly.
Whene'er the choice is up to me 10
I choose the ones that I prefer,
the tales which make me happier.
What gives the greatest pain of all
is that my choice is very small.
Though no one has a tale to tell 15
so fashioned that it suits me well
still I am light of heart and would
much rather tell you something good
than what's not right for me to say
and steals another's joy away. 20
So I'll relate a story such
as ought to please you very much:
   A noble had a lovely wife
who was as dear to him as life
and rightly so. She could surpass 25

the radiance of a looking glass
and was as fine as she could be.
Whene'er a wife, you will agree,
has beauty mixed with kindly ways
she well deserves our warmest praise.   30
She was so honorable and pure
her husband needed to endure
because of her no pain nor woe
and that is why he loved her so.
So perfect all her manners were   35
that there was never seen in her
a fault which one might blame her for,
which made him love her more and more.
To all his friends and guests she brought
a welcome, as a good wife ought.   40
Her mate could not at all compare
with her, for he was not as fair
as he'd have wished in face and limb.
I'll tell the simple truth of him:
his form was slight, his face was seared,   45
and to the others he appeared
a hundred years of age or more,
but didn't to his lady, for
she thought that Absalom could not be
as fair or Samson strong as he.   50
He was for her a man apart
and none but he could fill her heart.
'Twas nobleness that made her true,
but there were other reasons, too,
for all the things that anyone   55
could do for honor he had done.
He did them well, as if he were
as mighty as an emperor
and just as fair as any man
created since the world began.   60
He always had an open hand
with all his property and land
and any deed would undertake
for those he served for honor's sake.

That's why he traveled in and out 65
in all the countries round about.
   Now it occurred, as oft of old,
that the nobleman was told
of mighty battles going on;
and many comrades soon had gone. 70
He went along, for he was brave
and fought so well there that they gave
much higher praises to the knight
than to all others in the fight.
(Had he remained at home, you know, 75
with her, then you would need forego
hearing a single word from me
about his vaunted bravery.)
Since he performed the greatest feat,
it's not surprising he should meet 80
misfortune which did not befall
some others who throughout it all
were well behind and far away
(of them I've not a word to say).
From such a one he lost an eye 85
who saved himself and did not try
to fight with any other men
and envied him his courage then.
The noble's wound was deep and sore;
however, what distressed him more 90
was that his wife would see him so
and that the sight would cause her woe.
For he was pained by her distress,
and what pained him pained her no less.
   On the journey there came one 95
with him who was his sister's son,
given for training to his care.
He led him from the others there
and said: "Dear friend, now go from here
and tell my lady, sweet and dear, 100
my fate is such that, I believe,
I never more shall cease to grieve.
Before I was not fair to see,

but God has now so dealt with me
that I'm ashamed and cannot stand 105
to be in any German land;
I must depart and go alone
from countries where my name is known.
And tell my sweet one that my heart
will stay with her when I depart, 110
no matter whither goes my way,
and that I've never heard her say,
unconcealed or secretly,
a thing which showed contempt for me.
She's been too kind to speak amiss 115
and so has honored me by this;
may all the world indeed commend
her. Tell her what I say, my friend.
I cannot see her more — and you
must let her know that this is true — 120
no more her lovely form and face;
I'd be a cruel man and base
were I to live with her again.
She shall be spared this grievous pain.
Since I'm not worthy of her now, 125
no single day shall I allow
the sight of me to cause her woe."

   In tears the page set out to go
and soon arrived where he was sent.
The lady saw him there and went 130
and spoke and drew the boy to her:
"I've seldom seen a messenger
who's been so truly welcome here;
you'll not refuse me words of cheer,
my friend, about your uncle. Tell 135
me if my lord is feeling well."
The child was weeping as he said:
"He sends devotion in his stead —
whatever land he journeys to,
his heart will always stay with you. 140
This is no more than you've deserved,
for no fair lady ever served

with more propriety a knight
or one less pleasing to the sight.
He wasn't fair enough before, 145
but now a blow has made him more
unsightly so that, though he's wed
to you, he cannot share your bed
and now must say a last farewell."
The lady spoke then: "What befell 150
the one who means so much to me?"
The messenger replied: "Why, he
has lost an eye, and bravely, too."
The lady said: "Good friend and true,
go, bid him come without delay 155
and tell him, what I've heard you say
I do not like and cannot bear.
His pain is something we should share
and must, for we have but one life
and just one body. I'm a wife 160
who has a husband she can prize:
and if he had a thousand eyes
and each of them were fair and clear,
to me they could not be more dear
than is the one remaining still 165
which my heart cherishes until
it cannot know or has forgot
if it looks beautiful or not."
"Lady, I'll tell you, as I ought,
my journey back would count for naught; 170
so let me tarry here with you.
What he has said, he'll surely do;
no solemn word that he has spoken
to you has ever yet been broken."
"I would to God," the lady said, 175
"that I could take upon my head
his every sorrow and that he
were fair as he would like to be.
I hear you say, I must resign
the one whom I would keep as mine; 180
it's bitterness and grievous need;

without him I'll be dead indeed.
I beg that you will undertake
to see him once more for my sake
and let him have the gift I'll send.   185
I won't be long; so wait, good friend."
The dear one left him on the spot
and went into her room and got
a pair of scissors from the shelf
and stabbed them in her eye herself   190
so that it ran down o'er her cheek.
All bloody, she returned to seek
the boy. It gave him such a scare
that with both hands he tore his hair
and cried: "Alas forevermore!   195
I've never seen the like before!
Good lady, what is this, I pray?"
She spoke: "Go find your lord and say
that he should come and look at me,
and if for him I seem to be   200
too fair the other eye shall go.
This is because I love him so.
And should I ever criticize
because he doesn't have two eyes,
then he can say when I am done   205
that I too see with only one."
She spoke: "Go, messenger of mine,
and beg your lord that he resign
such fancies and come back again
to me. He'll never need complain."   210
The boy went weeping on his way;
he'd never felt such great dismay.
He raced his steed and hurried toward
the place where he beheld his lord.
He ran to him and, crying still,   215
soon told the knight of all the ill
that he at home had seen with dread,
and what the faithful wife had said
was quickly added to the rest.
The knight in sorrow smote his breast   220

and spoke: "Alas forevermore!
I should have ridden home before.
Alas that I was ever born!
My pretty wife has now to mourn
her eye. I wish that I were dead."
He cried aloud and from his head
pulled out the hair. A follower
rushed up and spoke: "Thanks be to her!
How well has she revealed to you
that she in every way is true."
The words struck deep into his heart
and strength and courage did impart.
"The man has told the truth," he thought,
"and how much dearer now she ought
to be, and is, since she has shown
this tenderness for me alone."
He told the courier: "Hasten back
and see that she does not attack
herself again with such a deed.
From early till late I too shall speed
to join my fair and faithful one
and tell her that for what she's done
to show her love and constancy
I'll do whate'er she wants of me."

He followed him and hastened there.
When he saw the lady fair,
with tears of love to her he ran.
The sweet and charming one began:
"My noble friend and husband dear,
I bid you hearty welcome here."
The lord then spoke with great dismay:
"O how can I, my love, repay
you for the great distress and pain
which I have caused you to sustain,
so wifely wife? What deed, alas,
is this that I have brought to pass?"
The good one said: "And if you now
would pay me back, I'll teach you how —
just trust my word that you indeed

 are all which I desire or need,   260
and love me also in this wise.
For if I had a thousand eyes,
and if I found they pleased you not,
then I'd care nothing for the lot."
 Who formerly with joy had gazed   265
upon the beauty all had praised
now liked to see her even more,
knowing the faithfulness she bore
her husband. This was fitting too
for she was beautiful and true,   270
a woman whom one well could prize
much more than some who have two eyes.
 To all the other faithful wives
may God give happy, carefree lives.
I'll let them know who spreads their fame: 275
Herrand von Wildonie's my name.

The Deceived Husband

(Der verkêrte wirt)

Strange tales, whoever wants to tell
them always ought to prove them well
or name some witnesses thereto;
for when the singer claims it's true,
a listener is apt to say: 5
none saw it happening that way.
Suspicion such as this
I hope now to dismiss
with simple truth and honesty.
The nobleman who told to me 10
this singular event
is one so excellent
and with honor so complete
that what I've heard the knight repeat
is something which I safely may 15
spread out before the light of day.
   Sir Ulrich, Lord of Liechtenstein,
whose knightly virtues ever shine,
told me this narrative,
that once a knight did live 20
in the country of Friuli.
(Since he's forgotten truly
to give to me the noble's name
I'll have to do with you the same.)
The noble had a wife and she 25

was beautiful as one could be
and very pleasing to behold,
her husband, though, was very old.
Upon a plain his castle stood;
behind it lay a pretty wood; 30
an oriel projected there
from the bedroom of the worthy pair.
Another noble dwelt nearby
the place, and he had fixed his eye
on this fair mistress with delight. 35
He really was a handsome knight
with gallant ways, the truth to tell,
which pleased the lady very well.
He served her eagerly, and so
she sent him word to let him know 40
how he would be repaid.
The knight was not dismayed
by this; in all his life before
no tidings ever pleased him more.
The messenger addressed him: "She 45
desires that you come stealthily
to her abode and that you stay
in the thicket. Ere the day
go beneath the oriel
and what you'll find will please you well, 50
for hanging there you'll see a ring;
in the bed above the string
winds around my lady's toe.
Pull this and she at once will know
that you are waiting there for her 55
and will come down to greet you, sir."

   That night the noble came and crept,
as planned, to where the lady slept.
He found a little ring of gold
hanging just where he'd been told. 60
He reached up, seized, and pulled the ring,
but then the husband felt the string
which lay upon his leg and pressed

now on him and disturbed his rest.
He would not wake his wife but did
desire to see what o'er him slid.
Silently he felt about
and very soon the man found out
just what the string was fastened to.
The other end he quickly drew
to him till it was in his hand.
And when he found the golden band,
the old man, startled, understood:
"My wife is up to nothing good."
His fingers let the ringlet go
which fell unheeded in his woe.
He sprang up swiftly from his bed
and hastened to a door which led
out toward this thicket which was near.
The noble who was waiting here
thought: "It is my lady sweet."
So when he heard from his retreat
a creaking door, he hastened there.
The husband seized him by the hair
and called for help with all his might.
The other thought: "If I should fight,
then talk will ruin her good name,
and I shall have to take the blame.
I can escape and save my life;
you didn't bring a sword or knife
with you, while I am here well armed
and have no need to be alarmed."
Startled by her husband's call,
the lady, who'd slept through it all,
got up and put a garment on
and thought: "Alas, my husband's gone
and found the knight who waits for me."
She hurried down unhappily
to where they struggled on the heath
with one on top, one underneath.
She spoke: "What's this? What is this now?
Dear husband, can I help somehow?"

"I'd like to know," he answered her,
"just who might be this visitor
who brings dishonor to my name." 105
She said: "You'll soon be free of shame.
Give him to me and get a light,
and if I do not hold him tight
whom you have given, I shall let
you have my head to square the debt." 110
The husband thought: "If she should go
to light a candle where I know
a dozen men are sleeping, I
might come to more disgrace thereby
than from the one whom I have caught." 115
He answered: "Take him, but you ought
to listen well to what I say,
for if you let him get away
I'll know that you're to blame, my wife,
that he is here. You'll lose your life 120
in place of him, and quickly too."
The lady said: "Whatever you
give me to keep while you are gone
I'll hold, and pledge my life as pawn.
He gave the knight to her and ran 125
to get a light as was his plan.
The noble spoke: "My coming here
will cause you great distress, I fear."
She answered: "Go and wait for me
there in the court." "It shall not be," 130
thus spoke the knight, "for, lady dear,
you've pledged your life to keep me here.
Before I'd go away and kill
you so, I'd die, and with a will."
She said: "Don't worry." With a kiss 135
he spoke: "God keep you safe through this."
What she did then I know full well
and what it is I have to tell:
the lady quickly looked around
and took a donkey which she found 140
by the ears. 'Twas not the kind

of beast nor in the frame of mind
to think it fitting, it appears,
that one should seize him by the ears.
The donkey backed away from her;　　　145
however thick the bushes were,
he backed up over them and through.
She thought: "If I let go of you,
my lord will think me guilty. I
must keep you as an alibi."　　　150
Thorns and nettles, many a bough
were no strangers to her now,
but close companions; with dismay
she saw them tear her clothes away.
Soon the lady was quite bare　　　155
and blood ran down her everywhere.
Then her lord came running out;
he hadn't wandered long about.
He brought a blazing torch with him;
the lady now was vexed and grim　　　160
that he'd been gone so long. Cried she:
"This thing may be the death of me,
unfaithful husband, which you told
me, when you went away, to hold.
He ran up panting in his haste　　　165
to share the danger that she faced
and give her aid. When with a gasp
he saw the donkey in her grasp,
he spoke, surprised and with regret:
"I wish that we had never met!　　　170
Speak up! What happened to the knight?"
She said: "Look here, I'm holding tight
to what you gave me when you ran,
as sure as you're the devil's man."
He answered: "Go to bed, I know　　　175
that you are false from head to toe."
He then retired. His wife sat near
the bed; as soon as it was clear
that he was sleeping, fully spent,
the lady left the room and went　　　180

into the courtyard and awoke
a friend of hers to whom she spoke:
"Go to my husband in my stead
and take a seat before his bed.
If he should speak, you must be still.   185
I'll soon be back; I swear I will."
"What have you done," her friend replied,
"that you're afraid to go inside?"
"We've only had a little row,"
the lady said, "I'll tell you now;   190
don't be concerned if he should hit
you several times. I'll pay for it
with half a pound as your reward."
The other thought: "Suppose her lord
should beat me; half would stop the pain,   195
and all the rest of it is gain."
She hurried there and sat before
the bed and softly closed the door.
The lady showed her favor well
then to the knight. I need not tell   200
you what they did so secretly.

   The husband woke and soon could see
his wife was not with him in bed.
"So you're still mocking me," he said.
No word. He cried: "Come here, be quick!"   205
She did not speak. He took a stick
and laid her down and beat her till
he thought that she would do his will.
He then lay on the bed to rest
and once more angrily addressed   210
her: "If you don't come here, I'll let
you have what you will not forget."
The woman thought: "If I should choose
to tell him who I am, I'll lose
the credit for the pain I've stood   215
and shall have nothing to the good,
as I should have. An unkind fate
has brought me to this wretched state."
He said: "If you don't come right now,

I'll come to you, and so, I vow,
that you will wish I were not there.
Again he took the stick to where
she was and gave her many a stroke.
"Tomorrow you may claim," he spoke,
"you didn't get a beating; hence
I'll let you wear the evidence,
which will be proof enough for me
that you have let that man go free."
He forced her to his feet and drew
a long, sharp knife. With no ado
he cut her fair hair with a stroke
off above the ears and spoke:
"I'm sure that you will never make
yourself more hair before I wake,
though you have proven that you can
make quite a jackass of a man."
His labors had been such a strain
that when he lay back down again,
the man collapsed and slept as dead.

   His wife had shown her love and said
farewell with many a fond embrace
and came to take the other's place.
She spoke: "Dear cousin, you can go.
I can appease him now, I know."
"All my appeasing," said the poor
attendant, "was a loss, I'm sure.
I don't know what you did to him,
but I've been through a penance grim
which I'll remember evermore.
No woman ever got before
so many frightful blows, I swear,
and then he cut my pretty hair
right off." The lady spoke again:
"Who never suffers any pain
enjoys no comfort. Know that I'll
be sure and make it worth your while."

   At this the wretched woman fled
back to her children. To the bed

the lady went and gently crept
close to her husband, who now slept 260
and did not know that next to him
his wife was lying, limb by limb,
her cheek pressed right against his own.
   When on his face the sunlight shone,
the husband woke and looked at her 265
and said: "If you had earlier
done this, you'd have no need to fear."
She spoke: "What do you mean, my dear?"
"I mean that you, you wicked wife,
have brought great trouble to my life." 270
"My lord, I haven't done a thing."
He answered: "Tell me, where's the ring
that by a cord hung to the ground
which on the other end was bound,
as I discovered, to your toe? 275
You're trying now to move me so
that I shall listen to your plea
and forget the trick you played on me."
She spoke: "How's that? What did I do?"
"You bade another come to you 280
and wait in the thicket there below.
The cord lay on my leg, you know,
and I awoke when he began
to pull. I went to find the man
and seized him as he waited there 285
and held him by the ears and hair."
She spoke: "What happened to your prey?"
"You quickly won the man away
and in a manner, wicked wife,
to make me hate you all my life." 290
"If what you say was really done,
what did I do with what I won?"
"You took the man from me, alas,
and gave me in exchange an ass
which you were holding by the ears. 295
You think me foolish, it appears,
but I'm too clever to believe

all that." "And what did I receive?"
she asked. "The answer's on your back."
She spoke again: "And if it's black   300
and blue you'll know the story's true."
She bared her body to his view
and said, "But if my back is white,
perhaps you had a dream last night."
"Now let me see your hair," he said.   305
"But why?" "I cut it from your head
to punish you." "My hero! Yes,
that's why you married me, I guess:
so you could always dream that I
did not hold honor very high."   310
He spoke: "You don't dare let me see."
She answered: "If it should not be,
then all is false which you relate.
Know this, you'll have my endless hate,
and I'll condemn you while I live   315
to every friend and relative."
He spoke: "That you would rage, I'm sure,
and I would have much to endure.
But you won't say a thing, I know,
if you don't have long hair to show."   320
She said to him: "Since you insist,
I'll let you look at what you missed.
Just see, I combed my hair so well
because of him of whom you tell."
With this she threw her cap aside.   325
"If I have lost my hair," she cried,
"'twill sadden him whom I'll display
it to this coming holiday."
So ample was the hair that graced
her that it fell below her waist.   330
The husband gave a start and thought:
"I've lost my senses and I'm caught.
What did I accuse her for!
And if my wife should nevermore
be kind to me, 'twould suit me right.   335
It's only what I earned last night.

How could it happen! What's it mean?
Damnation! If I hadn't seen
her untouched hair and body too,
I still would think it all was true." 340
He said: "Dear wife, I really had
no thought that you would get so mad,
for this was nothing but a joke."
"I wish you'd spare me," then she spoke,
"the games that try to take from me 345
my virtue and my honesty.
Just find a woman of the sort
who can enjoy this kind of sport."
"Dear wife, I'll give you something nice,
a mantle of the highest price 350
with baldaquin or velvet cloth,"
said he, "if you will not be wroth."
"Do that," she spoke, "and I'll refrain,
but never mock me so again."

We would not ever have found out 355
what all this trouble was about
and just what happened, were it not
that she who lost her hair and got
the beating finally betrayed
the lady, since she hadn't paid 360
a penny of that half a pound;
that's how the story got around.
And he who tells this history
is Herrand, Knight of Wildonie.

The Naked Emperor

(Der blôze keiser)

If you'll be still and listen too,
then I'll relate to all of you
a tale which once upon a time
I read. 'Twas writ without a rhyme,
and in the German tongue as well.　　　　　5
When I found what it had to tell,
it seemed remarkable to me.
A lady asked most tenderly
that I would put the tale
in verses without fail.　　　　　10
Because of her I rhymed it then,
and beg the ladies and the men
that they'll be kind and not make fun
of me if it is not well done,
but even think my work is good.　　　　　15
Could I but phrase it as I would
and serve her every way I know!
I love the charming lady so.

　　In Rome an emperor once reigned
whose power was more unrestrained　　　　　20
than any I have heard about.
His wealth exceeded far, no doubt,
what other monarchs have amassed,
and soon its measure had surpassed

all bounds and changed his heart and will, 25
as riches do with many still.
It raised to such a height his mind
he could not think that one would find
him ever suffering from need.
It caused him to believe indeed 30
that not a thing could happen which
would leave him otherwise than rich.
He thought his wealth would last forever
and could vanish never,
that his repute was such, 35
he'd be esteemed as much
even after he was dead.
And, if a child should be misled
to thinking thus, it could become
the butt of mockery for some. 40
So he, the strong and blind,
had failed to keep in mind
that Jesus Christ, our king,
is lord of everything
and, judge of each affair, 45
to joy or to despair
can hasten any man who lives,
according to the gifts he gives.
 The book recounts the tale this way:
Twelve Sundays after Whitsunday 50
the emperor had gone to where
the mass was celebrated there.
They sang it splendidly;
the monarch heard and he
(when it was over), with a nod, 55
brought to his side a man of God
to whom he spoke: "Before you go
tell me the Gospel we're to know
today." "I shall," the priest replied,
"God's words appear there as our guide. 60
The message which was sung to us
is written in Luke's Gospel thus:
'For who exalts himself shall be

brought low, and who is humble, he
is raised.' " The emperor was grim;
"Not so," he said, and glared at him
with angry passion, "That is wrong.
Whoever on this earth is strong
is mighty in the life to come.
What profit would I gather from
my honor and the work I've done
to earn the fame which I have won?
And if a poor man there were deemed
nobler and were more esteemed,
I'd have to be indeed ashamed.
I don't believe what you have claimed.
The story simply isn't true,
and he who told it lied to you."
"I'll say no more of my belief;
but see that you don't come to grief.
The story isn't true, you hold;
the One who tells it never told
a lie in all his years;
that which therein appears
is true in a life that's pure, and He
so gave Himself to purity
that He of all is best
and nobler than the rest.
Whoever lies cannot be pure.
No falsehood is so small, I'm sure,
that he who told it e'er could stay
with God in purity a day.
Since He could never justify
His creatures when they tell a lie,
a falsehood would be deep distress,
for lying is uncleanliness."
When this was said, the chaplain went;
the emperor did not repent.
   The monarch held no courts; at last
ten years without a judgment passed.
Therefore the empire's state
declined; its need was great:

since justice soon could not be found,
burning and pillage was all around,
as is still the case today 105
when justice and the law decay.
And then the emperor decided
to hold a court where he resided;
he bade the knights that they
announce to all a day 110
on which the monarch would
judge everything he should.
He also knew that it was wrong
for him to let this go so long
and that he might expect 115
God's wrath for this neglect.
The bailiffs spread the news at last:
in Rome when forty days were passed
the emperor would hold a court
and settle claims of every sort 120
which never had been heard.
Those who received this word,
both rich and those in need,
approved of it indeed.
Opposed were those alone 125
who at the time were known
by all to rob and thieve,
and one can scarce believe
they'd welcome this decree.
No, 'twas plain to see 130
the tidings did not please
in any way such men as these.
When the day was now at hand
there came the people of the land:
the greatest and the least, 135
the layman and the priest,
the friar and the nun;
who wanted justice done,
I fancy, he was there.
With them came many a lady fair 140
who surely would have stayed at home

had need not driven her to Rome.
  When the monarch heard that some
worthy ladies too had come
of noble birth and charming grace, 145
he thought: "Tomorrow I shall face
these pretty women. This is why
it would be well, perhaps, if I
should bathe and put on fresh attire
to make their lovely eyes admire 150
and also touch their hearts, of course."
The emperor got on his horse
and rode through town to where he might
obtain a bath so late at night.
He told his followers to wait 155
for him outside before the gate.
Within, to aid the emperor,
were three fine pages, but no more,
and several women of the kind
that one in such a place will find. 160
He bathed as other people do
and just as soon as he was through,
he said: "Now pour the water on.
We'll warm ourselves and then be gone
to where the knights and horses wait 165
for us to come, before the gate."
They heated so at his request
that he lay on a bench to rest;
the windows had been closed before.
Then a man walked out the door; 170
just like the emperor he came:
the voice and body were the same;
it looked like him in every way.
The chamberlains without delay
sprang up and gave him clothes and cloak. 175
"I'm truly sorry," thus he spoke,
"that I have bathed so long. I fear
you have grown tired of waiting here."
"No, lord," replied the retinue,
"it really wasn't much to do." 180

He climbed upon a steed and rode
to where the emperor abode.
The chamberlains then followed soon
with the clothing worn that afternoon.
Who played the monarch took his seat   185
with many noblemen at meat
and jested while they ate their fill.
   The foolish emperor lay still
upon the bench, well satisfied.
A bath attendant ran inside   190
the bathhouse and aroused him when
he spoke: "The monarch and his men
have ridden to his residence."
The pages wished to hasten thence,
and in a moment all were dressed.   195
They hurried after him, distressed
that he was in the castle now
and they'd been left behind somehow.
Attendants then began to air
the room; the emperor lay there   200
upon his bench and had to grin
that anybody should come in
and say that he had left the place.
"What do you want here, Sir Disgrace?"
a boy addressed the monarch thus,   205
"Perhaps you'd like to swindle us
ere dawn and take our clothes and such;
we wouldn't like that very much."
"Now bid my chamberlains," said he,
"bring clothing here; it's time for me   210
to dress and ride on home. I pray
that God protect you till the day.
I can't remain with you tonight
but fancy I shall do all right
or even better where I dwell.   215
Your raiment wouldn't fit me well."
The boy replied: "If I should heed
and go 'twould take me long indeed
to find what you desire. It's clear

that you've as many men this year 220
as last. Your robes or chamberlain
God knows that I would seek in vain
in here, because there's not a stitch
of clothes or sign that you are rich;
and none would guess to look at you 225
that you had wealth and retinue."
"What can this be?" the monarch thought,
"They do not know me as they ought;
I'll have to go myself and see.
If no one's waiting there for me 230
with clothing at the door, 'twill go
quite hard with certain men I know."
The emperor looked out the door
and found there no one waiting, nor
was anybody in the road. 235
But further off, near his abode,
he heard a lot of sound
and noticed torches all around,
borne here and there to light the way.
He also heard some people say 240
the emperor was dining then.
He thought: "Great God, what have I been
throughout my life? What can I claim,
since everyone confers my name
on someone else, and here I stand 245
as one with neither wealth nor land?"
He wondered what he ought to do.
His haughty spirit caused him to
be too embarrassed to remain
and so he ran inside again. 250
The bath attendants said: "Go now,
and you can save yourself a row;
for, if you do not, you may get
what you will certainly regret."
"My friends," the naked man then cried, 255
"just let me stay with you inside,
for God's sake; and you need not fear
that I would think of doing here

a thing to cause unhappiness.
My heart is full of great distress." 260
They spoke: "You should have told indeed
the monarch all about your need
when he was here just recently,
for he could help you more than we.
Now go." The naked emperor 265
at this went weeping out the door;
behind him they made fast the gate.
He stood there in a wretched state:
some twigs were all the clothes he had
to cover him, and he was glad 270
that night had come to hide his shame.

When the woeful outcast came
into the street, he crept
from place to place and wept
till he had reached the city's end 275
and there it was he saw a friend
before a castle where he'd stayed
at times, a counselor and aid
to whom he always had been good.
He thought: "If anybody would 280
be able now to rescue me
from care, I think it would be he."
He ran but found the gateway barred
as always by a castle guard
whom he asked to let him through. 285
The man said, "I'd be crazy to
and let you vagrants enter thus;
it would go hard on both of us.
You'll have to stay outside, for sure;
fools my master can't endure." 290
"Good man, then go to him," he said
"and bid him come to me instead;
you need but whisper in his ear
the emperor Gorneus is here.
That I've been good to him, he knows; 295
now he can pay the debt he owes."
At once the old man hurried toward

the place where he would find his lord.
"My master," so the guard began,
"before the castle waits a man 300
who says, and is quite serious,
that he's the monarch Gorneus
and sent me here. He added too
that he had done a lot for you.
He's sure a naked majesty; 305
my finger's no more bare than he."
"I'll come with you," the master spoke,
"to see this man, just for a joke."
The lord walked out before the gate
to where the other had to wait. 310
He saw him, naked and ashamed,
and to himself the lord exclaimed:
"Dear God, the man who stands before
the gate's just like the emperor;
his body and his hair, 315
his face and general air
are like those of my lord renown.
Had I not left him in the town
just now at meat with friends about,
I'd think this he without a doubt." 320
The naked man then spoke: "My friend,
I've come to see if you will lend
me some advice; my want is great,
for things are in an awful state.
Remember all that you possess 325
because of me; your faithfulness
should help me in this time of need."
The lord said: "Who are you, indeed?"
"Why talk like that?" was his reply,
"Your monarch, Gorneus, am I, 330
who's really done a lot for you.
You know full well, I wouldn't do
as much to please another, for
you've been a favorite counselor
to me and such shall you remain 335
when I win back my power again."

"Just go away," the lord spoke then.
"I left my ruler with his men
just now inside his castle, far
across the town, but, since you are   340
so like him, take the coat of gray
the servant has and run away.
And if you use once more this name,
you'll get no pleasure from your claim."
"My strongest hope," the poor man said   345
regretfully, "at last is dead."
   He ran back to the town with dread
and went about to beg for bread
from kitchen boys. They showed their spite
and said: " 'Twould only serve you right   350
if you were hanged, since you won't soil
your hands with any sort of toil,
although you surely don't look weak.
You're just as bright of hair and cheek
as any girl could be.   355
You'll get no charity,
but only what would go to waste;
we hope that it will suit your taste."
The scraps of food thrown at his feet
were all he got that night to eat;   360
he ate till he could eat no more.
The morning afterward he bore
the water to the kitchen, though
he didn't like it, that I know.
Whenever he would stop to wrap   365
his shoulder, he would get a slap.
He heard: "You glutton, you," when beaten,
"you'd like to sleep when you have eaten.
It well may be your laziness
at last will cause you great distress.   370
Perhaps you're proud because of your
resemblance to the emperor?"
This question made him so upset
he always broke out in a sweat.
He didn't like to be thus named;   375

it made him very much ashamed.
   As soon as the morning meal was done
and he was sitting by the one
with whom he'd borne the jug that day,
he heard the kitchen master say 380
the emperor was holding court.
When the wretched man got this report
he thought 'twould be a blunder
should he not see this wonder:
"I ought to know who this can be 385
who's using my authority."
At once he walked across the square
and saw that many a person there
had lost his head as punishment;
he heard much wailing as he went 390
from women and from men.
He noticed others then
against their will led by the hand
whose eyes were covered with a band
of cloth. He saw that some were tied 395
upon the wheel and loudly cried.
Many a head of noble stock
that day was laid upon the block
and wicked fools for evil guile
were burning there on many a pile. 400
Among the dead were quite a few
whom he had liked and nobles who
would not have been condemned a bit
by him whate'er they might commit.
When he beheld the justice wrought 405
upon them, to himself he thought:
"Thou, Lord God of might,
hast given, as was right,
my place to one who isn't vain
and knows how emperors should reign. 410
I should myself have been the one
to do this. What I've left undone
another carries out. I can
expect but hatred from this man

who strives for honor thus, and fame. 415
For this I merit only shame,
since all my lifetime I've done naught
but reap the good that fortune brought,
and no one else thereby has gained;
because of this my heart is pained. 420
Whatever pleas the poor have made
were set aside by silver paid
into my coffers. This was used
to make accusers the accused.
Their plaint has reached God's judgment place, 425
and I've become the world's disgrace.
He's judged their suits in such a way
that I have suffered great dismay.
True were the charges made therein;
I now confess to Thee my sin, 430
Lord God, and ask for grace alone.
I'll always labor to atone
and do whatever is Thy will.
I know Thy love is greater still,
however great may be my crime. 435
What I have done until this time
Thou canst forgive and wilt, I know,
that I may ne'er again act so."
He thought then: "Surely, if I can,
I ought to go and see this man 440
who reigns in place of me, whose hands
have seized my government and lands."
He went to stand before the gate
and slipped through when the press was great.
He pushed as humbly as he could 445
into the throng until he stood
almost at the front and gazed
upon the judge whom all had praised,
and rightly too, for one could find
virtue in him of every kind. 450
The poor man looked at him with care
to see what likeness might be there;
he watched at length and saw that they

were as alike in every way
as if it were himself. He knew 455
he could not blame his retinue
at all, nor did he think it queer
(so similar did they appear)
that folks believed the man was he.
He thought: "Besides, he seems to be 460
so noble that, were one to choose,
he'd surely win and I would lose
compared to him, and this is right.
All things are equal in God's sight,
Who rules o'er those in heaven so 465
as He would have us reign below."
The best of clothing one could get
from any royal cabinet
were on this noble judge renown,
and also the imperial crown. 470

  The virtuous one then addressed
the princes there: "May I request
(if it may be) that you allow
me to go to my chamber now;
'twill be a little while before 475
I come to sit with you once more.
But let a prince assume this task
for me and give to all who ask
a judgment that's without caprice.
The princes answered, "Go in peace, 480
for God's been with you all the day;
indeed, the people rightly say
that ne'er before has anyone
seen justice as today was done."
They helped him from his seat. He went 485
to where the wretched beggar bent
his head to watch him through the crowd,
the one who'd been a monarch proud.
He took the latter by the hair,
then led him to his chamber there 490
and after them made fast the door,
which scared the poor man even more.

The lord said: "Why do you look thus,
O foolish monarch, Gorneus?"
The poor man fell upon his face 495
and wept and spoke: "Lord, grant me grace;
I am not, nor can hope to be
the emperor, for you are he."
The master said: "Now say if you
can now believe that it is true 500
that Jesus Christ, our Lord and King,
is ruler over everything
and humbles whom he would make low,
and that He's able to bestow
all gifts to those who persevere 505
and rightly strive for honor here,
Who made you rich in wealth and fame,
and Who now lets you suffer shame?
God gave the honors which you mourn
and now exposes you to scorn. 510
You once believed that lofty state
was yours because your power was great,
but, as you see, your might is small,
and God alone rules over all.
You turned your chaplain's words aside 515
and claimed that God Himself had lied.
Whoever taught you such a thing?
Speak up, for God's the very spring
of virtue and of guiltlessness.
You wretched simpleton, confess 520
that He has given you the wealth
that you possessed and fame and health;
for this you always should fulfil
whatever service is His will."
Before his feet the other lay 525
and wept with sorrow and dismay
at all the sin upon his head.
"My lord, be merciful," he said.
"To you, and God as well, I own
the great disloyalty I've shown 530
to my Creator up till now;

but, if you give your help, I vow
to do whatever you advise,
because you know me and are wise."
"You've made confession as you ought," 535
he spoke, "and shown you can be taught;
so stand up now and be restored:
I am an angel of the Lord.
This royal clothing you must don,
and don't forget from this time on 540
to turn from all which is not right
and finds no favor in God's sight.
How good to you the Lord has been
and better than to other men
to make you wiser than you were! 545
Take my advice and do not err,
and you will live in majesty,
both now and in the world to be."
When this was said, the seraphim
placed his royal robes on him 550
and took the golden crown he wore
and put it on the emperor.
When this was done, he spoke again:
"You have your country and can reign
and use your power as you would. 555
Take care that you be wise and good
to all and rule as God would do;
that's why He sent me here to you."
He fell down at the angel's feet
and spoke: "Dear master, I entreat 560
you, be with God my surety
that I will follow each decree
of His, and gladly, from this day."
With this the angel went away.

   The emperor returned to meet 565
the princes at the judgment seat.
None interfered as he sat down,
for he now wore the royal gown
of him who'd just been sitting there.
And was he toward the poor more fair 570

than he had been ere he found out
what they endure? Oh yes, no doubt.
   Twelve days the monarch heard the suits;
when he had settled all disputes
he asked the populace to go. 575
He told the princes then: "I'll show
that I can rule as you desire,
and you'll be glad to call me sire.
I ask that you will have appear
without delay before me here 580
the ones to whom I've given pain.
I shall not let them go again
until their wrath has been dispelled.
To him whose legacy I've held
unlawfully, whoe'er he is, 585
I'll give back everything that's his.
If any tariff I've collected
should be unjust, 'twill be rejected,
for profit gained thereby is wrong.
I'll coin no money for as long 590
as you think best and wait indeed
until the people feel a need.
If you have evil statutes, too,
they must be altered, and by you."
The princes spoke: "Lord, good and kind, 595
we praise our God because your mind
is turned toward Him, as it should be;
therefore we'll follow your decree
more readily, you may be sure,
from this time on, both rich and poor." 600
So then the emperor did what
he'd promised them, right on the spot:
his riches he began to share,
and so that all the people there
were glad when they departed thence. 605
   He went back to his residence
and sent to get those who had been
more helpful than three noblemen:
a bishop and an abbot gray

and his confessor too were they. 610
The monarch spoke: "You now must aid
me with advice; although I've paid
all those who brought a rightful suit
(and this was done without dispute),
I've still a lot left over now 615
and have decided to endow
cloisters and priories with it,
for I don't want to keep a bit.
I got it wrongly, and the toll
was such I nearly lost my soul. 620
Because of this I'll nevermore
become as wealthy as before.
If you approve of my intent,
it's how the money will be spent."
They answered: "Master, no one knows 625
a counselor who'd dare oppose
a wish like that, nor why he would.
He'd earn God's anger if he should."
"Then take it," thus the monarch told
the three. "I'll give you all my gold 630
and silver; it is quite a lot.
I shall not keep a thing I've got
but what is rightly mine alone.
Each day I'll also share my own
for God and for the empire's need. 635
I'll live that at my death, indeed,
the devil shall not linger near,
nor after I depart from here."

Thenceforth the emperor so reigned
that men and women both maintained 640
he must be holy, through and through,
and what they said was really true.

I pray to God that He impart
through him such wisdom to my heart.
Lord God, Thy virtue didst Thou show, 645
Thy power in this world below,
by dealing with the monarch thus.
He once had much, but Gorneus

lost honor with his raiment.
He then received in payment 650
enough of both while still on earth.
Thou madest him so learn Thy worth
that he obtained by what he'd done
the best that man has ever won:
Thy paradise, O Christ, and prize. 655
Since Thou art virtuous and wise,
reveal in me Thy virtue now;
this favor may Thy will allow
because of her on whom I call,
the closest one to Thee of all 660
(Thy noble mother whom we love).
For those whom Thou art fondest of
on earth here or in paradise
so work that I from every vice
and all my sin may here be free 665
and may fare well eternally.
This is poor Herrand's prayer and cry;
the Knight of Wildonie am I.

The Cat

(Diu katze)

A cat lay peacefully and dozed;
upon an oven she reposed.
Her husband too was there, but seized
with restlessness and sore displeased.
He looked him over here and there   5
and spoke: "Another beast as fair
as I may well exist at that,
yet I'm still living with this cat.
Powerful and bold am I;
I am agile and I'm sly,   10
handsome, full of pride.
Were I satisfied
with her who's lying here, my wife,
I'd surely fret away my life
with things to do and see   15
not good enough for me.
No female is so fair or wise
that she'd not think me quite a prize.
I'll go and seek for love anew.
May God (without me) care for you!"   20
   Where could he find a wife, he thought,
with beauty such as that he sought,
with power and from a noble race.
He thought: "I'll go no other place
than to the sun, for she has might.   25

Her shining gives the world its light."
He spoke to her when he came near:
"I haven't seen in many a year
a bride whose beauty is so great.
If you will have me as your mate, 30
I promise, you're the one I'll wed."
"Now tell me more," the sun then said.
"How did you come to this desire,
and why is it you don't acquire
a wife who better suits your kind? 35
"I'll tell you what is on my mind:
I want a wife whose power is such
that nothing else has near as much."
"With your permission," spoke the sun,
"I would propose another one 40
whose strength excels my own indeed."
The tomcat cried: "It's she I need."
The sun continued: "When I rise
and stand in power in the skies,
there comes along with mighty force 45
a fog and hides without recourse
the brightest, most majestic shine.
Her power must be more than mine,
that you yourself can understand;
go there and ask her for her hand." 50
The tomcat spoke: "Indeed I'll go;
you won't object to this, I know.
For, if such wondrous gifts belong
to her, she really must be strong."

    The tomcat left. When he could see 55
the fog, he spoke respectfully:
"God grant you honor, lady true;
in loyalty I'll stay with you,
for I would take you as my bride."
"But tell me why," the fog replied. 60
"I want a woman, I confess,
who has such might as you possess.
By strength and beauty I was drawn

to seek the sun, she sent me on
to you and told me, what is more,
what I can never praise her for.
She said that you were stronger yet
than she; a fact that I regret,
for I'd been happy to remain."
"What made you go away again
is something which will never cease
to take from stupid men their peace.
If you must have a wife that's stout
and mighty, I can help you out:
the wind is much too strong for me.
However high or thick you see
me lie on vale or mountain top,
it will not ever let me stop,
but drives me on till I am brought
to where my former power is naught."
"I'll journey on," the tomcat said,
"for once again I've been misled."
 He found the wind was full of might.
He spoke: "I come with great delight,
to you, my lady, great and kind."
The wind said: "What is on your mind?"
"I'll tell what I've been thinking of:
no woman can I ever love
but her whose strength is never spent.
When I was at the fog's she sent
me forth from her without delay
and said, if I would only stay
with none but an aristocrat,
and one who's powerful at that,
then really you should be my choice.
And now that I have heard your voice,
I know your might is not a joke."
"Since you're a man," the wind then spoke,
who seeks a wife who's good and strong,
I'll show you her for whom you long.
She lives not far away, and she

is mightier than three of me.
A lonely wall is standing near
against which many and many a year
I've blown my best and stormed away, 105
but she repels me to this day.
She cares not for my power at all
and knows I cannot make her fall."
He answered with astonishment:
"I'm quite surprised that you should vent 110
your rage on anything in vain.
I'll have to journey on again."
He sought the wall without ado
and said: "I'm glad to meet with you,
since your renown and worth are great. 115
Just now I heard the wind relate
what I cannot believe. You seem
too calm to merit such esteem.
Can you be powerful as well?
I'd not have thought, the truth to tell, 120
to hear the wind sweep o'er the land
that you could possibly withstand
its strength for just a summer night.
But she has told me of your might,
that for a hundred years right there 125
you've faced her and without a care.
Since you have stood so long before
her storm, I'll stay forevermore
with you and take you as my wife."
"That I should stand here all my life," 130
the wall said, "doesn't mean I'm stout.
A tiny beast is hereabout
who has more strength, I must admit;
I can't defend myself from it.
It's made a thousand holes in me, 135
and there's no way that I can see
to save myself. You can decide
from this if I should be your bride.
It's mistress here and I'm its house.

To tell the truth, this very mouse
has pained me more than ever could
the wind, before which I'd have stood
for many generations still.
But it has made me feel so ill
from top to bottom with its power
that I could fall within the hour."
"My journey," thus the tomcat spoke,
"were you its prize, would be a joke;
a sickly wife's not what I need.
Although the mouse is small indeed,
her strength makes her the one to wed.
How oft misfortune works," he said,
"to deal my marriage plans a blow,
and I may often suffer woe
before I've searched through every land.
But tell me now," was his command,
"where can I find the one I seek?"
The wall replied: "Just take a peek.
She's lying in her chamber here."

 The tomcat looked in full of cheer.
He said: "God bless you, Lady Mouse;
I've come to take you as my spouse,
and I am just the man for you.
The wall has pleased me through and through,
for she has told me something I
was glad to hear, and that's no lie.
She said that you were really stronger
than she, so I'll not journey longer.
I'll take you; just come out." "Oh no,"
replied the mouse, "that I'll forgo
and don't intend to leave this hole;
but if a worthy wife's your goal,
my mistress is the one, not me."
The tomcat spoke: "Who might that be,
that I should leave you for her sake?"
She answered him: "I always take
great care whenever she's about,

and I'd be lost should I come out,
for she would seize me right away.
I've hidden here the second day 180
with not a thing to eat or drink,
since I'm afraid of her, and shrink
before her awful teeth and claws.
I wish that you'd move back because
you make me think of her I fear. 185
The similarity is clear."
The tomcat said: "I'd like to know
the creature I resemble so;
I fancy you invented it."
The mouse spoke: "No, lord, not a bit. 190
She looks just like you; that is right,
though I can't say, because of fright,
much more of her — from whence she came
or what she's like — than that her name
is Lady Cat. But just to tell 195
you this has made me quite unwell."
He answered: "Since it gives you pain,
you need not say her name again;
I've known the lady well of late.
And can she be the perfect mate 200
whom I not long ago despised?
My scorn was really ill advised,
for she was noble and was kind.
That pride and folly seized my mind
is something I may suffer for. 205
How can I look at her once more?
But I am sure she won't disown
me: in the past she's always shown
such faithfulness and modesty.
She seems much better now to me, 210
for, since I felt I should despise
her, I have gotten much more wise.
It may be she can understand
that, even had she been more grand,
I'd not have stayed on as we were. 215
What drives me back again to her

is that the others do not care
for me. If I am welcome there,
it means that she is virtuous;
she's not obliged to treat me thus. 220
What kind of greeting shall I hear?
I'll have to suffer, so I fear,
a lot of scorn from her, and smart,
before I show what's in my heart.
And I am fearful, I admit, 225
that she's forever free of it.
I'll go to her, no matter what,
so wish me luck and quite a lot."

   The tomcat went to where reposed
the female cat, who lay and dozed 230
where he had often seen her lie.
He spoke: "How fortunate am I
to find again my rightful wife
with whom I ought to spend my life."
She said, and looked him in the face: 235
"I think that that might be too base,"
and lay back down upon her bed.
With great dismay the tomcat said:
"Now let me speak ere you decide."
"Have you been faithful?" she replied. 240
"We'll see what proof you can present;
but tell me first just how things went.
You were so handsome and so strong;
did someone tie you with a thong
to keep you where you traveled to 245
when I wasn't good enough for you?"
He spoke: "I had a thong to deck
me out on this disloyal neck.
The thong was faithlessness; but cease
to scold, and let us make our peace. 250
Forgive me; I have done you wrong,
although you cared for me so long.
But I remember now a creed
which comforts in my time of need
(I speak the truth, as well I might): 225

that mercy's better still than right."
The tabby said: "Were I to do
as you have done, I'd be untrue;
but there's no use to make a row,
since I can see you're sorry now. 260
We joyfully forgive the one
who rues the evil he has done."
 To all who find this tale is good
I say that everybody should
be grateful for the lord he's got. 265
Should he attempt to change his lot
he'll certainly have cause to mourn,
though the new one may be higher born
and richer than the former lord
with whom he lived in full accord. 270
For with another, it is plain,
the man will have to start again
and serve him well until the day
the lord is pleased in every way.
Had he remained with him, content, 275
with whom so many years were spent,
why then the lord would not ignore
the services he'd done before.
Who'd serve a stranger for the prize
of power isn't shrewd or wise; 280
for it's the master who is strong,
and this won't help the man for long,
but well may bring disdain, though he
may serve him very faithfully.
When such offense continues on, 285
and he can see how things have gone,
he leaves again; but it's no use,
because once more he gets abuse.
When he has traveled here and there
a while, the man remembers where 290
he spent his childhood years. Dismayed,
he thinks: if I had only stayed,
I still would have my faithfulness;
perhaps they'll take me nonetheless.

He journeys home, and should he find 295
the lord to be of such a mind
to take him gladly as his man,
he ought to serve as best he can,
and give up his excessive pride,
and let these cats become his guide. 300
This counsel Herrand gives to you
(von Wildonie they call him too).

THE SONGS

1

Lovely Summer, all the blooms have now
been destroyed and all the meadow's green
by the winter. This we must allow,
though he takes the beauty we have seen.
He's so furious and strong,
and the little birds have found his time is much too long.

But his rule is not so strict that I
won't increase your pleasure with my art
and from unrestrained delight sing high;
thus it is that mind can teach the heart.
Fool, this I cannot fulfill.
But were pangs of love to leave me, I'd sing better still.

Who seeks honor and supports the right,
who is always faithful to a friend,
him I'll ever praise with all my might,
wishing him good fortune to the end.
Man or woman, none the less,
honored be their names, may they grow old in happiness.

2

The Maytime and its beauty — these
have come once more
and the sunny days, so cheerful and so long.
The birds sing pretty melodies;
just as before,
from the sweetest nightingale I hear a wondrous song.
It's happy that the field and wood
and all about with splendor shine,
as I am glad this love of mine
is so fair and good.

Oh, if my fortune were so rare,
and could it be
my delightful one might give me such a fond embrace
that it would cause the lady fair
to fall to me,
then all my sorrows would be gone and joy would take their place.
Accord me, Minne, one request
and let me come so close to her
that she'll not scorn her worshiper.
This would please me best.

My lady's charming, not a flaw
does she possess,
and her beauty's too complete for any fault or stain.
Minne, let me see with awe

her loveliness,
for this would quickly free my longing heart from every pain.
Her little mouth is rosy red,
her cheeks are white with pink below,
untold the graces she can show.
Thus my love is fed.

We must all be light of heart,
both the ladies and the men.
Sorrow, you will soon depart,
for we've reached the season when
May's bright glow is seen, and heard
singing in the forest glades the voice of many a little bird.

They rejoice because the sun
rises from the hill anew.
What compares with even one
rose aglitter in the dew?
Nothing you could ever find
but a lady who is fair and also womanly and kind.

Love comes through the eyes when she
enters in the heart to woo.
Love to love speaks secretly:
"Dear, when can I be with you?"
        [line missing]
A little bird beside the forest sang to you this melody.